Thank you for your interest in learning about the OPTIC(S)™ System to solve the problems plaguing your business where people & process intersect.

Do you struggle with any of the following problems in your business?

1. Broken handoffs between departments
2. Process gaps bleeding money from your P&L
3. Frustrated employees, customers, and leaders
4. Poorly defined and undocumented processes
5. Unclear accountabilities and responsibilities
6. No system for streamlining work streams
7. Desire to get organized & standardized

These are the top seven reasons I have observed that great businesses fail to scale!

Interested in learning a system to solve these problems in your business? Scan the QR Code above or visit **OpticsBook.com** to begin your journey of eliminating the process problems holding you back!

You will find many additional resources, including case studies, tools, templates, and videos to support you on your journey.

Align People and Process
to Accelerate Performance

OPTICS

OPTICS
Align People and Process to Accelerate Performance

Copyright © 2024 Ryan C. Weiss

ISBN (hardback): 978-1-964046-28-0

OPTIC(S)™, OPTICS™, QVS™, and ARM™ are trademarks of
Effective Performance Strategies.

Expert Press
2 Shepard Hills Court
Little Rock, AR 72223
www.ExpertPress.net

Editing by Caroline Banton
Copyediting by Lori Price
Proofreading by Geena Barret
Text design and composition by Emily Fritz
Cover design by Casey Fritz

Align People and Process
to Accelerate Performance

OPTICS

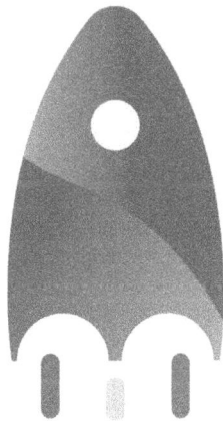

RYAN C. WEISS

Contents

Foreword

I recently had the pleasure of meeting Ryan Weiss through mutual connections. We have since engaged in fascinating discussions on the parallels between rocket science and engineering and the systems that make businesses and organizations function efficiently.

Ryan's first book, *From Orangutan to Rocket Scientist: How to Lead and Engage Your Team Through Effective Process*, explored his P5 Rocket theory and was the precursor to this current book, *OPTICS: Align People and Process to Accelerate Performance*.

As a former NASA rocket scientist, I appreciate the analogy of the P5 Rocket and the theory that systems and processes must align with your people for optimal functionality. The five Ps of Ryan's rocket theory are: *P*urpose, *P*roduct, *P*erformance, *P*eople, and *P*rocess, and I wanted to briefly address these from the perspective of my rocket science days at NASA.

Ryan's five Ps illustrate why OPTICS is such a relevant system to apply whether you are working on space exploration with NASA, launching a startup, or seeking to improve your business operations.

Purpose

If I go back to my time at NASA, it was critical to define the *purpose* of what we were trying to accomplish. Each part of the organization had a defined sub-purpose that fed into the overarching purpose or mission. Whether you have to wake up 11,000 people to solve the Apollo 13 explosion in space or launch the space shuttle, it's a monumental task to coordinate teams in California and Maryland, manufacturing teams at the Cape in Florida, and mission control in Houston to launch and return a spacecraft without losing it. Each team in each location has its own sub-purpose that feeds into the overall mission. It's a similar situation in the corporate world, although arguably, the scope and stakes are not as high.

Fundamentally, in either scenario, you have potentially thousands of people in place moving the organization in the same direction of growth. In Ryan's analogy of the P5 Rocket, purpose is portrayed as the nose cone of the rocket. The nose cone must point in the right direction with the product, people, and processes all aligned so that the rocket can reach its destination. But there are a million calculations and tasks to do along the way to make sure the trajectory stays on course.

Alignment starts at the top, at the nose cone. When the space shuttle exploded during its launch in 1986, everyone looked to NASA for an explanation, and the director of NASA was ultimately responsible. Everyone at NASA was serving the director. NASA was the client, and having a common direction driven by the head of NASA was critical to the mission. The purpose of the mission or the organization has to filter down so there are no competing factions that can drain resources or make the mission unsafe.

Product

The product of a mission or organization can also be described as the payload. It's the value created by whatever work is being done. In the early days of the space shuttle program, the goal was to launch satellites into space and, ideally, have a reusable spacecraft that could return. Since then, satellites have brought us the ability to map and monitor Earth, predict hurricanes, and monitor fire pollution, air quality, and pollution in the water. Similarly, companies create value for their stakeholders, and they are constantly innovating to create new value.

Performance

One problem we experienced with NASA regarding shuttle missions was what I describe as the problem of "how to put ten pounds of sugar into a five-pound bag." We were collecting millions of data points during a shuttle launch, all of them critical. We needed to monitor the rocket systems, computer systems, atmosphere, and even the health of the astronauts down to their heart rates. We needed early warning systems to tell us if there might be a potential malfunction. And these all had to be microsecond and millisecond calculations because when the space shuttle was traveling at 17,000 miles an hour, it doesn't take much for something to go wrong. We had so much information, but we only had so much computer capacity.

In the corporate context, organizations must also find ways to monitor key metrics like sales volumes or telemarking center call volumes, and they have to monitor and take care of their employees through career development to ensure high morale. Organizations must monitor their inputs, outputs, and everything in between to enhance performance and avoid disasters.

One of my favorite movies is *Apollo 13*, which tells the story of the thirteenth crewed mission in the Apollo space program and the third crewed mission attempt to land on the moon. The craft was launched from Kennedy Space Center on April 11, 1970, but the lunar landing was aborted after an oxygen tank in the service module failed two days into the mission.

There's a scene in the movie where the astronauts are monitored by ground control and are told, "Okay, it's time to flip the switch." The astronauts comply and immediately feel an explosion. Ground control has no idea what happened, nor do the astronauts. It takes some time for the communication to get to a point where the astronauts and ground control can understand the data and find the problem. The systems are out of alignment.

One of the assignments I worked on at NASA was running flight simulations to test the responsiveness of the equipment and the thousands of people working on launch, orbit, and reentry. We had to test every feasible outcome to verify that both the equipment and people could respond and return the space shuttle and astronauts safely.

Simulations are so important because you must also look at your environment, and in the case of business, the market forces. You must do simulations to predict problems and find solutions before they occur. Of course, you can't plan for every scenario. At NASA we didn't simulate a tile falling off the space shuttle, and when it happened, it blew us away.

People

At NASA, the environment was one of constant monitoring and management in a changing environment. The teams and different players involved were vital. I mentioned how we monitored the health and vital signs of our crew and used that data to stave off any potential problems with the astronauts, but we also monitored our external actors.

The value of external actors was brought home to me when I worked for a manufacturing company that designed and built a laser-sighting device for tank guns during the Iraq War. An overall contractor built the laser-sighting gun, and we were responsible for a small component in the gun that handled the laser-sighting equipment.

At some point, the laser was misaligned. It was also causing injuries. The situation was so severe that the company's contract and those of the other manufacturers were going to be cancelled, and rightly so. We needed to solve the problem. We spent six months simulating the climate and war environment in Iraq and testing the equipment in a room controlled for humidity, temperature, and local conditions. We discovered the problem lay with the type of glue that was being used in the manufacturing process. One of the suppliers was trying to save a nickel on a gallon of glue and was supplying a subpar product.

This is an example of how important it is for organizations to not only manage their teams but also their vendors and suppliers. Without a joint relationship and a shared vision that is understood, a mission can be sabotaged. In our case, one actor's decision to save pennies on a gallon of glue cost lives.

Processes

People rely on processes. If astronauts can't rely on a key process, or if they don't trust that something will happen to the thrusters when they flip a switch, they're going to find an alternative way to function, which may have disastrous consequences.

Another movie I love is called *Hidden Figures*. It depicts the story of a team of three female African American mathematicians who served a vital role in NASA during the early years of the US space program when they were first sending John Glenn into space.

The NASA teams were relying on computers to do the calculations to determine where the exact landing spot would be when Glenn returned to Earth.

They needed to locate the aircraft carrier at that spot. When Glenn learned about the reliance on computer algorithms, he said, "I'm not comfortable with that process. Make sure it is backed up by human calculations as well."

The movie is a reminder of how important it is to have processes in place that are consistent. And if you do need to make changes, which you will, there have to be consistent metrics to show that what you are trying to accomplish really is going to work.

Propulsion – Human Energy

When you are at T-minus ten days and ready to launch, it's too late to start thinking about your people and processes and how well aligned they are. Now you have to focus on propulsion. For propulsion, you need fuel and oxygen, or in an organization's case, human energy.

Now is the go or no-go decision. Do you have the right product for the current market? Launch too early, and people won't adapt to the user interfaces. Launch too late, and you lose out to competitors.

In the rocket science world, there is also max Q to consider. Max Q is the moment of maximum pressure in a shuttle takeoff. It's when all the engines perform consistently to get the power and thrust to move forward. If you get past this point, you know the launch is successful. And it's no different from an organization launching a product.

This book goes beyond P5 Rocket theory and finesses Ryan's approach with a pioneering concept called OPTICS. The OPTICS system ensures that businesses and organizations gain clarity and alignment in their processes so they can execute their business strategies. This book is rocket science for business, a blast to read, and contains a motherlode of valuable insights.

—**Dr. John E. Knight,**
former rocket scientist for NASA

Introduction

What do NASA, SpaceX, business owners, and leaders all have in common? They all need alignment between people and processes to realize their mission. When launching a rocket, engineers know exactly which questions to ask prelaunch and what the right answers should be. They have meticulously honed their checklists and processes to ensure the best outcome. They have identified the ultimate human expertise in terms of scientists, engineers, and astronauts. They have aligned their people and processes to enhance performance.

OPTICS is the system that fuels your P5 Rocket ship (organization) and accelerates its performance. I've helped hundreds of businesses across a variety of sectors align their people, processes, and products. That work has culminated in OPTICS, a system used by organizations of all sizes to align people and processes toward accelerated performance. The principles apply across businesses regardless of scale and sector. Service industries, construction, distribution, and manufacturing—whatever your business size or model, OPTICS works.

This book explains what the OPTICS system is, why it works, how to execute it, and what business leaders and entrepreneurs can expect from the system. The book includes practical self-reflection exercises and templates showing how the OPTICS software and process works. The exercises are an opportunity to apply OPTICS within your own contexts and operations so you can begin to develop your own framework and uncover how to optimize alignments of your people and processes.

You don't need to be a rocket scientist to use the OPTICS system, and it won't take you to the moon. However, in just six hours, you can determine the direction and propulsion you need to get your business where you want it to go.

—Ryan Weiss

Are You Ready to Launch?

Why Choose OPTICS?

OPTICS ('äptiks) has two definitions :
1. The study of sight and the behavior of light.
2. The way in which an event or course of action is perceived by people.

This word was selected carefully and thoughtfully to represent the intersection of people and process that organizations need to navigate for success!

For any organization to accelerate its performance, its people and processes must align. Having talented and motivated people along with well-engineered processes leads to great things. I have developed the OPTICS system over many years. You will find the principles apply across businesses

1   https://www.oxfordlearnersdictionaries.com/us/definition/english/optics

regardless of scale and sector—service industries, technology companies, and manufacturing. Whatever your business size or model, OPTICS works. I have never seen the process fail to turn a company around and find itself better organized and higher functioning.

I'm not asking you to take my word for it. I'm suggesting you read this book to discover what OPTICS is and how it works. I also invite you to visit the interactive audio-visual experience at www.epsoptics.com, where you can get a taste of all that OPTICS offers for your organization. Try the self-reflection questions I have included and apply the OPTICS concept to your situation to decide if this system is right for you.

First, I'll give you a synopsis of the OPTICS system and an explanation of why you should try it.

Nearly every company has:

- Employees who rely on other people, departments, and external parties for information
- Suppliers it can count on
- Customers who expect to receive information, parts, or products

The OPTICS system provides a framework for identifying all these groups and connecting all the dots, both internally and externally, so each person involved in any part of the process can understand what they need from others and what others need from them.

Only with this clarity and understanding of their own role and how that fits within the overarching purpose of the organization will people use processes in the correct way, without taking shortcuts, missing steps, and creating chaos.

The OPTICS system is not just for organizations that are failing. Any individual or organization can benefit from this approach regardless of your current situation or stage of growth. That said, I have identified seven scenarios where OPTICS really shines.

Seven Scenarios Where OPTICS Shines

OPTICS can be applied to an organization at any stage of its development, but the following seven situations serve as context for an explanation of how OPTICS can help organizations navigate inevitable changes:

1. You have outgrown your processes, and your business has become larger or more complex. In other words, what got you here won't get you there. You might need to:
   a. Open a second office
   b. Expand to a new state
   c. Launch a new product line or service

2. You are undergoing change management, such as:
   a. Implementing a new inventory, accounting, CRM, or ERP system (software platform or update)
   b. Restructuring your leadership team
   c. Facing a merger or acquisition

3. You are experiencing changes in market dynamics, such as:
   a. COVID disruptions or other forced changes
   b. Economic conditions prompting organizational change

4. You are coping with employee or leadership turnover by:
   a. Realigning accountabilities and responsibilities
   b. Onboarding new employees

5. You are preparing to scale by:
    a. Gathering documentation for franchising or licensing
    b. Planning for expansion or growth

6. You are seeking and implementing operational efficiencies (streamlined processes).

7. You are seeking a strategic management system:
    a. For a startup
    b. For an established and growing company

1. You have outgrown your processes.

As your company evolves, it naturally outgrows its processes. If you open a new office, your operation becomes more complex by expanding into new markets. If you launch new product lines or services, your business model becomes more complex. If a single entrepreneur decides to scale and hire employees, things become more complex.

When such changes occur, the initial person or group of people needs a different structure within which the new people can function, apply new ideas, or create and deliver new products. Sometimes changes occur gradually and organically, which gives everyone and everything more time to adapt. In other cases, such as a merger or acquisition, changes can come quickly, and there may be significant resistance to new people and processes.

Recently, I worked with a $2 billion packaging company that was the result of one company acquiring two others in a relatively short period of time. It was really three companies with different cultures and systems all trying to work together under one umbrella. The three core business units were not aligned in terms of doing things cohesively. There was some synergy between them, but few common processes connecting them together.

At some point, all companies need to examine how the different groups of people in their organization are functioning and find a way to bring them together in a common language. The OPTICS system will help you do exactly that.

2. You are undergoing change management.

Aligning people to processes entails examining the habits of those involved, but habits are notoriously difficult to change.

Companies are constantly undergoing changes of some sort, and systems and processes are designed to keep things in order. While a reorganization, merger, or leadership change are all traumatic experiences for a company, sometimes even a simple change can create chaos. Here's a case in point and an example of how OPTICS turned things around:

Case Study: The CEO and the New ERP (Enterprise Resource Planning) System

In 2018, I received a call from a business owner. The owner and CEO was operating ten warehouses in various locations across North America from which the company rented equipment for construction projects. The owner's father founded the company, and when the daughter took over the helm, four or five warehouse locations had already been established. Because things were going so well, the owner opened five additional locations. She also implemented a new software platform, which was supposed to solve problems but instead created chaos!

The company's staff was composed mostly of people who had been with the company for decades. They had developed habits and behaviors that worked with their legacy systems. They were not prepared for the new software system the CEO introduced.

No system is perfect, and over the course of time, the employees had created workarounds for problems they encountered with their existing system.

The existing system worked despite being somewhat patched together; the teams were able to service and invoice clients and make sure the company was paid for those services.

When the new CEO implemented the new software platform, the company failed to do due diligence considering how the new system would disrupt their teams. Worse, there was no thought given to ensuring new workarounds if the software implementation didn't go to plan. Basically, there was no plan B.

The day the CEO called me, things were bad, and she was in a panic.

"Ryan, I don't know what inventory I have or where it is. The system isn't tracking what's happening with the inventory. Can you help me?"

After some conversations, I discovered that she had implemented a new inventory management and enterprise resource planning (ERP) system. The system used new, handheld barcode scanners, but the employees didn't know how to use the scanners properly, and the scanners weren't consistently linking to the ERP system.

Part of the reason for implementing the system in the first place was to be able to use the handheld and mobile scanners at customer sites and at the company's own locations. This proved difficult because the company was delivering inventory to construction sites with metal buildings that didn't always have good cell phone coverage and didn't support the use of the scanners.

Critically, when problems with the scanners occurred off-site or on-site, with no plan B, the employees had no workaround or alternative system; there was no paper documentation either. The old system had already been disabled.

So, there were three main problems with the new system:

1. The scanners weren't configured properly.
2. The scanners didn't consistently connect to the software.
3. The employees did not have a backup plan for when the problems occurred.

Under normal conditions, if a scanner didn't work on-site, the delivery person would put the item in the truck, deliver it to the customer, and try to figure it out later. But this was the company's busy season, everybody was running full speed, and the system had very quickly started to fall apart.

Using OPTICS, a team composed of myself, the CEO, and key personnel, identified the core process steps of the rental delivery operation. We systematically listed out the sequence of events that occurred for a delivery. For example:

1. An order is received from a customer.
2. The order is processed.
3. The delivery date and time is set.
4. The delivery is completed and the product is installed.
5. Upon completion, the equipment is picked up.

At each step in the process, we knew that the inventory had to be updated because it was critical to know what rental equipment had been delivered where and for how long. Using OPTICS, we mapped each of the key steps of the rental delivery operation and started to identify the inputs, the outputs, and the people involved in the process. These three components of an operation must align if a process is to be optimized or even successful.

One of the challenges the owner was struggling with was that she felt her business was different from other businesses using the same software, and she was right. Her business was different because every business is different. But by understanding the new software, the old process tool they had used before, the people using the tools, and the habits and behaviors they had developed, we could begin to break down and simplify the process in a way that allowed the new software to align with the people using it.

The OPTICS system acted as a framework for sorting through the mess and having everyone involved come together to create a clearly documented way of changing dysfunctional operations to highly functional ones.

Five years later, the owner of this company is still a client of mine. Throughout the COVID-19 pandemic and ensuing disruptions, we continued to work at aligning the habits of her employees with the new system so they stay on the right track when new challenges emerge.

Aligning people with processes entails examining the habits of those involved. Almost always, changing processes requires changing habits, but habits are notoriously difficult to change. In the case of the CEO and the new ERP system, people had to form new habits, such as using new software and new scanners and coping with the addition of new offices and new teams.

The OPTICS system uses a framework that enables people to start seeing their habits and understand **why** they need to change. Usually, habits need to change so teams can collaborate. Sometimes, different departments just toss things over the cubicle wall or to another department and say, "Well, I don't know what to do with this. See if you can deal with it."

When the service department in the case study found that the scanners weren't working, they just made the delivery and left a voicemail with the admin department hoping that somehow the delivery information would make it into the system. You can see how well that went.

3. You are experiencing changes in market dynamics.

The COVID-19 pandemic caused incredible changes in all aspects of business life. One of my clients was completely disrupted by COVID. The company changed from an in-person business model to a completely virtual business model within a matter of days. Using OPTICS, we successfully took their existing processes and converted them into new, highly functioning processes, engaging the entire team in the transformation.

Before we implemented OPTICS, the employees were completely stressed out. When we worked through the initial OPTICS framework, they were so fed up that they were reluctant to do what we were proposing. It was enough for them just trying to get through each day.

Below are the before and after results of working with the employees over a six-month period.

On a scale of 1-5, how did you feel at the beginning of the year?

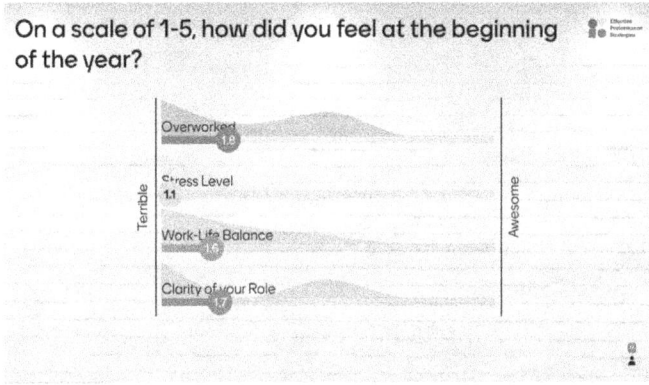

Terrible — Awesome

Overworked — 1.8
Stress Level — 1.1
Work-Life Balance — 1.6
Clarity of your Role — 1.7

On a scale of 1-5, how do you feel now?

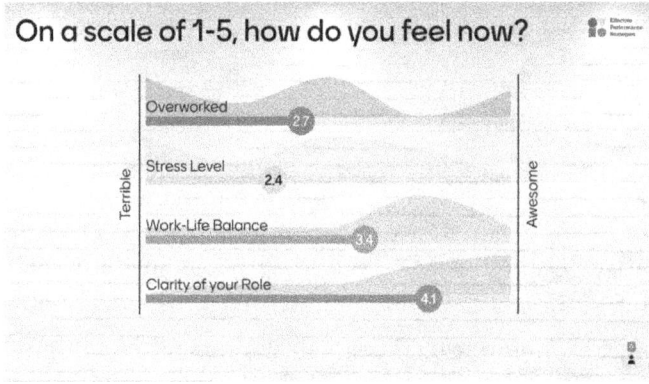

Terrible — Awesome

Overworked — 2.7
Stress Level — 2.4
Work-Life Balance — 3.4
Clarity of your Role — 4.1

As we walked them through the OPTICS system, the employees opened up and began to gain more clarity in their work roles that helped to relieve some of the stress they were experiencing. After we implemented the framework, we recorded an improvement of two to three times in employees' perception of their stress levels and work-life balance.

Changing operational dynamics can be a good thing or a bad thing. But what's critical is to set a strategic direction based on the anticipated changes. To use a cliché, "to pivot." Some companies thrived during COVID because they were able to adapt their manufacturing processes and make masks. Other companies had to completely reorient themselves just to survive.

The OPTICS system forces companies to look at their current situation, define where they want to go in the future, identify the gaps, and map out a plan to get there.

4. You are coping with employee or leadership turnover.

Strategic planning is most often done at the leadership or board of directors' level, and the goal of strategic planning is to maximize the use of a company's core processes and resources amid changing market dynamics.

Many companies approach planning and the processes from an internal perspective. They look at what is going on in their factory, shop floor, warehouse, or operations as though it's a vacuum. Companies often struggle to approach strategic planning from a holistic point of view. Consequently, there is often poor alignment with disparate groups operating independently. Silos are created with their own processes and no coordination between them.

It's important, then, that an organization's leadership group of an organization evaluate its end-to-end value stream so long-term goals and values are not abandoned when board members leave as well as not needing to go back to the drawing board. Those members who have been with the company for a long time understand the people and processes from the ten-thousand-foot perspective and can keep the ship on course during changing market dynamics.

Mergers and acquisitions (M&As) are characteristics of changing market dynamics, and they create disruption at the leadership level. People leave organizations during the upheaval of M&As, and the loss of institutional knowledge can be devastating. One company I worked with lost someone with thirty years of experience. There had been no attempt to preserve the knowledge the person had accumulated; it remained all in their head.

You can't put a value on institutional knowledge and experience. OPTICS can help preserve institutional knowledge and mitigate the problems that come with turnover at any level.

5. You are preparing to scale.

For companies that want to scale by offering franchises, acquiring other businesses, or growing in other ways, OPTICS can help develop clear lockdown systems that franchisees need to execute a new concern. The OPTICS system organizes, documents, and systematically applies processes and procedures to ensure consistent branding and execution. In doing so, the OPTICS system helps you prepare for growth. Before growth occurs, the framework identifies and assesses gaps and puts the right foundation in place before you jump in with both feet.

6. You are seeking to streamline processes for improved operational efficiencies.

Almost all organizations have room for operational efficiencies. Efficiencies occur when teams collaborate better and share institutional knowledge. The OPTICS system builds a framework or system to make that happen.

You will experience significant improvements in terms of communication and mutual understanding between departments, identifying areas for automation and laying the foundation for future improvements. I've seen the OPTICS system bring together people from sales through to production by giving them a framework for clear communication with which to address common pain points. The various departments work together to solve them and no longer operate in isolation. This is actually one of the most powerful elements of the OPTICS system.

7. You are seeking a strategic management system.

In its most basic form, OPTICS is a strategic management system. If you're a startup, an established and growing company, or a much larger organization that needs alignment and a fresh approach, OPTICS is fundamentally about bringing people and processes together, identifying performance gaps, and accelerating the growth of the company.

If you are experiencing any of the challenges outlined above and are looking to create an exceptional road map to coach your team, automate workflows, and assess the integration of AI to enable your team's growth, then you are in the right place!

Workbook: Reader Self-Reflection

In this self-reflection section, I recommend asking yourself some questions to help clarify what OPTICS can do for you. I've asked these questions to hundreds of executives, and their answers create a focus on their own lives, processes, and alignments. Also, please take notes in these sections as we work through the book.

Question 1: What pain does your organization feel when processes break down?

_____

_____

_____

_____

Question 2: What pain do your vendors or suppliers feel when processes break down?

_____

_____

_____

_____

Question 3: What pain do you experience when people don't follow your processes?

_____

_____

_____

_____

For question 1, consider how your internal organization suffers when your processes and handoffs between departments break down. What are the effects on employees and operations?

Next, consider what would result if you could remove that pain for your employees. What would happen? What could your organization achieve if your problems were resolved?

For question 2, think about how your external stakeholders, investors, and vendors are affected when your processes break down.

Next, if you could fix the problems, consider whether your employees, customers, and investors would be happier. Could you scale your business and be more profitable?

For question 3, when employees, colleagues, or customers don't follow the processes, how does that impact you? Do you lose sleep?

Do you experience situations where employees figure out a workaround because the processes aren't working? Perhaps employees do this without your knowledge because they are afraid of losing their job or the biggest customer.

What pain do you feel when those workarounds create even more chaos? If you could remove that pain, would you feel more fulfilled and more content?

To help you in this exercise, here are some answers given by past clients.

- "When people fail to follow the agreed-upon process, disorder can prevail. If everyone is doing things their way, rather than one best, optimal way, additional steps are required. Ten different ways of doing things causes extra work, leading to frustration."
- "The pain I experience is the additional time we need to spend reversing what was done incorrectly, maintaining process credibility, and ultimately retraining the individual who is not following the process."
- "The pain I experience is anxiety about inconsistency or being out of compliance."
- "When people or organizations don't follow processes, things are missed or fall through the cracks."

Key Takeaways

- The OPTICS system enables you to align people and processes to accelerate the performance of your team and eliminate broken handoffs.

- Business leaders define performance in terms of profit, speed, or efficiency. The OPTICS system enables you to achieve greater performance in all these areas.

- OPTICS alleviates the pain felt by your customers, employees, vendors, and, most importantly, you.

2

What Is the Ultimate Result of OPTICS?

Clients I have worked with have all experienced the following results from OPTICS:

- Improved execution
- Increased profitability
- Scalable growth
- Reduced costs

Don't take my word for it. Let me explain the OPTICS system in detail so you can decide for yourself if you think it can benefit you and your organization.

There are three elements that occur as the OPTICS process unfolds, and these three elements combine to create stunning results.

The Dynamics of OPTICS That Create Results

The three elements created by OPTICS that underlie its success are *clarity*, *simplicity*, and *alignment* in your business operations.

Clarity

If your employees don't have clarity in their roles, they often freeze with indecision. For example, if an employee is responsible for a certain task but doesn't know exactly how to execute the task, doesn't understand the scope of the task, or, most critically, doesn't understand the purpose of the task, then they may freeze with indecision, do the wrong thing, or even do nothing at all.

The employee might decide to execute the task thinking it's the best thing to do, but the impact of that decision on other people involved further down the line could be severe. Critically, if an employee does not understand the purpose of a task, they may take shortcuts that are not helpful. The shortcuts they take may actually create chaos because their lack of understanding causes them to make poor choices that create ripple effects later in the work processes.

Customers and suppliers also need to have clarity. If a customer is not given adequate information on how to use a new software product launched by a technology company, they will not use it successfully and will feel frustrated. If a new coffee shop opens but the ordering process is too complex, a new customer may well feel uncomfortable and go to another location.

Your supplier and vendors need clarity on what they are supposed to deliver, where they should deliver, and how they should deliver it. Without clarity, an order could be shipped to the wrong location, arrive late, and ultimately cause chaos for your company, which frustrates your customers because they can't get what they want. So, clarity has ripple effects throughout the value chain. (I once had a client receive a truckload of aluminum at their corporate headquarters in the middle of a large city!)

Simplicity

During a meeting, my client and I thought we had come up with a tool and a process that would improve his operations. The client was the CEO of a training company for hair salons and stylists. After hours of fine-tuning our idea, he looked at me and said, "This is too complex; my trainers won't use it."

Make everything as simple as possible, but not simpler.

We were developing a process together to better align the owner's operations with his customer journey—his customers being the hair stylists he trained. We had been brainstorming and developing the process for a while, but he realized, as did I, that it was too involved and training people to use the tool was going to be difficult. It was not viable or scalable.

"You're right," I said. "It's too complicated."

We tore up the process and took a step back. We asked ourselves what was needed out of the process and how we could achieve it in the simplest possible way. Albert Einstein once said, "Everything should be as simple as possible, but not simpler."

We applied that concept, which is a loaded one if you think about it. It's easy to make something as simple as it can be, but if something is missing that is essential to the process, then the process is too simple, and it will no longer work.

Mouse traps illustrate Einstein's concept well. The old-style traps are composed of some peanut butter on a block of wood, a spring, and the trap component, which is a lever with a connector. If any one of those parts is missing or broken, the mouse trap won't work, right? It's a simple contraption, but all the pieces must work.

Now, contrast that simple mouse trap with the epic board game *Mouse Trap*, where players construct a highly complex system. The engineering works great if every moving part functions, but there are so many moving pieces that the potential for failure is much greater. The point here is that if your operations and processes are complex with unnecessary or additional layers, you are not setting up your customers or employees for success.

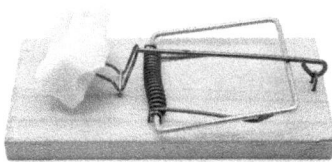

In the mouse trap analogy, the traditional, simple mouse contraption delivers the desired result far more effectively and efficiently.

Elon Musk applied the philosophy of "first principles thinking," coined by Aristotle. Aristotle believed we learn more by understanding the basic principles of a subject. Going back to the drawing board to get to the root of the problem can help problem-solvers see an issue under a different light.

One reason electric cars were unpopular twenty years ago was that batteries were expensive while gasoline was plentiful and cheap. What was the point in using an electric car? When innovating with Tesla, Musk boiled down the problem of expensive batteries and asked himself:

1. What materials are used to make batteries?
2. Who sells those materials at the lowest price?
3. How do you make a battery?

Using first principles thinking, Musk found a way to buy cheaper materials and create batteries himself at a lower cost.

But even if a business owner has clarity and believes their process is super simple, there is one more critical component for a process to work: people. Someone has to be willing and able to execute the process. Otherwise, the value of clarity and simplicity is lost. Only when all three components are aligned—clarity, simplicity, and alignment—will the process work.

Alignment

Even if an instruction is a clear statement on how something is to be executed, an employee may not follow the instruction. The purpose or meaning of alignment is to bring people into the process so they are engaged and ready to execute. Only when this is achieved will the results be higher profitability, higher scalability, and other metrics that an organization is trying to achieve.

Going back to the case study of the construction machinery rental agency, this case study illustrates well the concept of alignment and its convergence with clarity and simplicity. Regarding clarity, the company had introduced new software that was creating confusion because the users of the tool were not clear about their role, what they needed to do, or what steps to take if the handheld scanners and ERP system didn't work. This lack of clarity led to a situation where the company was unable to track its inventory and ultimately serve its customers.

The CEO's vision for the new software was for the machines to be scanned predelivery on-site at the warehouse and when delivered to clients. However, the CEO felt that her business was different from other businesses using the ERP. She believed her operations involved additional complexity because her business also installed and refurbished equipment in addition to delivering it. These different services were adding to the chaos of the software program's failings.

In fact, when we broke down the company's operations, we found that the business was no more complex than other businesses using this same software platform. We deconstructed the operations so they were as simple as possible *but not simpler,* and identified the key things that had to happen no matter what for her systems to function and her customers to be served.

In this case, there were four critical elements to a successful customer service job:

1. The receipt of a customer's purchase order for a machine installation with confirmation of payment.
2. The equipment had to leave the shop or warehouse.
3. An invoice had to be sent to the customer.
4. The equipment had to return to the shop or warehouse for service or refurbishment.

There were nuances, of course. For example, we focused on on-site installations, but there were cases where the machinery or equipment was just delivered to the customer who installed it themselves. Or a customer might come to the shop and pick up the machinery. Even in those cases, the critical thing was that every time a piece of equipment left the shop, a record of where that equipment was going had to be in the system. Then, every time a piece of equipment came back to the shop, there had to be documentation that it was returned to the shop and from where.

First principles thinking told us if the company had those two pieces of information, it could accurately invoice its customers and know where their equipment was located.

The additional complexities of on-site versus client installations were nice-to-haves, but it was additional information, not critical information. What was essential to running the business was knowing when a piece of equipment left the shop and where it went, and when it came back to the shop, where it had been, and when it arrived.

Once we understood the critical factors, we developed what we called a "garage door model." Every time something went in or out of the garage door, we had to know where it was going and where it came from. Starting with that, it became much easier to build on the other elements. For example, if we knew where the equipment had gone or where it came from, it was possible to add in service charges and additional fees, service calls, and other components of the business operations. So, simplicity became absolutely critical to rebuilding new habits and behaviors for everybody on the team.

The final piece for the company's turnaround was alignment. We had figured out with clarity what everybody needed to know and where the information needed to come from. We mapped it out with the OPTICS process and broke it down to the events that needed to happen every single time.

For things to be aligned, everybody on the team needed to have the same understanding of what they were to do and what was expected of them. They needed to know what the absolute bare minimum requirements were and how they should execute on them. And they needed to be on board and willing to create those new habits. In a short period of time, we were able to fix what was broken.

The software was not perfect, but it was not the problem in this case. The problem was the *way* the company was trying to use the software: The way that they were trying to get their people to use the software was so confusing, the workers gave up trying. In fact, the software could do almost everything they needed it to do if the people used it in the right way and if the software was configured appropriately to enable the people to do it. This is an essential part of the alignment of people and processes.

Had they rolled out the software after comprehensive training and the users knew what to do and how to work the system, and if they had launched it after testing, the situation might have been different. However, because the software still had configurations that weren't completely aligned with the business, and the workers didn't quite know how to work around those challenges, the software launch was a recipe for disaster.

So, to review this case, the first principles approach allowed us to identify just four basic things that had to happen for customers to be invoiced accurately, which gave clarity. We then configured the software to function so just those four things could be accomplished, which gave simplicity. Finally, we trained the users of the software on the basic functionality so the four goals were achieved.

By breaking down the processes, changing behaviors, and adding the complexities back in, the CEO was able to continue scaling her business. She opened new offices and explored other opportunities for continued growth and expansion. Without clarity, simplicity, and alignment, her business would most likely have failed.

Workbook: Reader Self-Reflection

What results would you expect in your business if your people and processes were better aligned?

_____

_____

_____

_____

_____

_____

_____

Key Takeaways

- Clarity, simplicity, and alignment are the foundations of OPTICS and the reasons it creates results.

- If employees do not have clarity in their roles, they may freeze with indecision, take shortcuts, or make bad decisions. Customers need clarity on how to use your products and services, and suppliers need clarity regarding your needs to serve you effectively.

- If your operations and processes are complex with unnecessary layers, you are not setting up your customers or employees for success.

- Alignment brings people into your processes so they are engaged and ready to execute. Without them and the correct alignment, profitability and scalability will be out of reach.

3

What Is the OPTICS System?

In a nutshell, OPTICS is a framework for clarity, simplicity, and alignment of your people and operations. It also brings fast results. Time and time again, I have transformed businesses for clients in just six hours. After three two-hour sessions working with OPTICS, it's possible to gain clarity and see your business through a sharper lens. With sharper vision, you can see where to make changes to better execute your operations.

In those first six hours, OPTICS can create a road map with deep levels of detail. It's that deep dive into your operations that brings clarity, allowing you to break down your processes into simple steps, and then work toward alignment.

I like to use the following analogy to describe the initial process of OPTICS. Imagine that in the first two-hour session of OPTICS, you are looking at your operations through a telescope. You are seeing the whole picture of your core processes from a ten-thousand-foot view.

As the sessions progress, depending on the scope of the project and what you want to achieve, you begin to look more closely at specific operations. You might focus on your customer service or finance department or your client onboarding process and consider the interactions between these processes and the rest of your operations. You are still at the ten-thousand-foot view because the objective is to first create a high-level map of what is going on within your organization.

Once you have this high-level view, you can now zoom in on problem areas. To do so, you look at your operations through a microscope, which gives you a greater level of detail. With this closer examination, you can pinpoint areas of misalignment, bottlenecks or dysfunction, or simply where things need to function better. At the microscopic level, OPTICS allows you to build a road map to fix those problems and align your people and processes.

Too often, people try to jump to the microscopic level to fix problems without first establishing an overall picture from the telescope. For example, a company might create a standard operating procedure for a task without an understanding of how that one procedure impacts other processes, departments, or people.

The concept of OPTICS is to take the opposite approach. It brings clarity to the big picture before drilling down on problem areas.

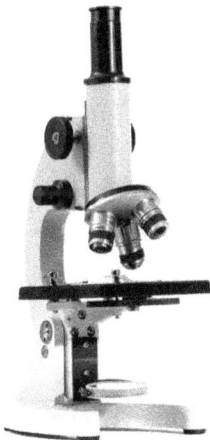

The final part of the OPTICS process is solving problems using individual job breakdowns, which I will go into later. The job breakdowns are ultimately how your people and processes become aligned. OPTICS provides the context and insight to solve specific problems at the job level because it reveals how specific problems interact with the bigger processes of your organization and what you should do about them.

Stage 1 of OPTICS: Preparation—Defining the Scope, Purpose, and Existing Gaps

The initial steps in the OPTICS process define three things: the *scope* of OPTICS, the *purpose* of OPTICS, and any existing *known gaps* in the areas of focus.

The Scope

Some preparatory work is required for OPTICS. Before the first two-hour session, we need to know the scope of the exercise. The scope of the OPTICS process can be high level. For example, examining all your operations as a whole would be a high-level application of OPTICS. Alternatively, you might want to focus on just one operation, such as customer service or procurement. This would be a lower-level application of OPTICS.

As well as determining the focus of the OPTICS exercise, the scope should also define where the process or operation to be examined starts and where it ends.

Let's say a company wants to focus on its customer service process. The scope of OPTICS in this case might begin when a customer places an order and end the moment the invoice is issued to the customer. The process would include the entry of the order into the system, the alerting of production that an order is required, and confirmation of delivery.

The Purpose

Before the OPTICS exercise begins, the goal of the exercise also needs to be defined. Why is the process to be examined in the first place? Suppose a company has a problem with its customer service. The problem is customer orders are incorrectly placed. This is causing frustration among customers. In the case of customer service, if a customer order is incorrectly placed, the customers will be upset, production wastes their time, and there is no payment. The goal in examining the customer service process is to reduce the number of customer orders that aren't fulfilled and improve the system.

The Gaps

Finally, before starting OPTICS, it's important to identify any known gaps that currently exist in the process under examination. OPTICS will reveal these gaps as the process unfolds, but it is better to define them as soon as possible because they may explain other anomalies that become visible.

For example, in a sales process, if orders are frequently entered incorrectly, that's a known gap. If clients are mistakenly invoiced for the wrong quantity, that's a known gap. If a client does not receive confirmation when their order is received and in process, that's a known gap.

The OPTICS system will focus on these gaps, examine why these gaps occur at each step in the process, and generate ways to eliminate or minimize them.

In summary, the first steps or elements of the OPTICS system are to define the scope, the purpose, and the gaps that already exist.

Stage 2 of OPTICS: Building the SIPOC (Suppliers, Inputs, Process, Outputs, Customers)

The second stage of the OPTICS process is the building of the SIPOC, which is the meat of the exercise. The SIPOC is built using the software and breaks down your processes both on paper and digitally. The result is an analysis of how your processes are aligned or misaligned. To build the SIPOC, each process is listed out under headings. The template below shows the headings: Suppliers, Inputs, Key Process Steps, Outputs, and Customers. The SIPOC uses metrics to measure the value of each key process step. I'll elaborate on the metrics later.

Suppliers	Inputs	Key Process Steps	Outputs	Customers
Step 8: Identify the suppliers of the inputs.	Step 7: Identify the inputs that are processed to create the outputs.	Step 2: Identify the first process step. This should be the first action in the scope.	Step 6: Identify the outputs of each step.	Step 5: Identify the customers of each step.
		Step 4: Write the final action step. This establishes the scope.++		
NOTE: Suppliers may be departments, individuals, or external suppliers.	NOTE: Inputs may include tools, parts, information.	Step 3: Write the final action step. This establishes the scope.	NOTE: Some outputs may be undesirable, such as waste or defects.	NOTE: Customers can be internal or external.

The SIPOC lays out each process step one by one, details its function and value to customers, and identifies its value in terms of quality, cost, and speed. The SIPOC also assigns accountability to each process step.

It won't be clear to you yet, but building the SIPOC enables your team to clearly see the logical connections in your processes and those causing employee frustration, waste, and missed handoffs. The SIPOC is the beginning of the road map for you to change these processes and connections to improve employee frustration and increase customer satisfaction, retention, and value creation.

To begin filling out the SIPOC, list each process step under the column heading, "Key Process Steps."

Next, for each process step, we define the suppliers and customers. This does not necessarily refer to external suppliers or the final customers. The customers could be external or another internal department team, such as operations, supply chain, finance, or sales. The customer might be an external customer receiving an order confirmation or a vendor the company needs to alert so they can receive information by giving them enough lead time.

In short, the customer is the receiver of the product of the process step, and the supplier is the party that supplies what is needed for each process step.

Here are the steps for filling out the SIPOC:

1. List the key process steps.
2. For each row, identify the customers of the process step.
3. For each row or process step, identify the suppliers of the inputs for that process step.

If you're interested in learning more about creation of the OPTICS system, check out the videos and other resource material at www.opticsbook.com.

Case Study

I have created hundreds of SIPOCs with clients during my career. However, one that stood out was a SIPOC created for a Chinese diaper manufacturer, Everbeauty Corporation. The SIPOC focused on Everbeauty's manufacturing operations. I facilitated the SIPOC process in English because I don't speak Chinese, but the conversation was translated into Mandarin and then translated back to me in English. I asked the CEO and his team questions, and we walked through the manufacturing process together, filling out the various columns and rows. On a whiteboard, we created the one-page SIPOC.

At the end of the first session, we had created a one-page SIPOC outlining the company's manufacturing operations from start to finish. All of a sudden, the complexity of the diaper manufacturing company was simplified and laid out. All of the operations were broken down so the connections and people involved could be seen. No one had been able to provide such a clear and logical perspective of the company's core processes before.

Through the translator and in Mandarin, the CEO said to me, "You understand my business better than anybody else in my company."

I hope this case study illustrates how the SIPOC takes complicated, layered, and interconnected processes and breaks them down to create clarity and simplicity. The process can be done at any organizational level, from the operation level with production facility operators to the strategic level with the C-suite. Creating a SIPOC will bring insights into how your systems, people, and processes are interconnected so problems can be solved.

Stage 3 of OPTICS: Building QVS

The third stage of OPTICS is to build the QVS. I stumbled onto the concept of QVS, which stands for quality, value, and speed, when I was in the Philippines managing a team of almost 200 people. At the time, I was managing various teams and sub-teams, and I was trying to develop a common framework of metrics to be used to improve the opportunities in each of the departments.

As I grappled with identifying meaningful metrics, I created a simple matrix for each department. I asked the representative of each department to identify one area where they needed to improve quality, value, or cost. For QVS purposes, value and cost are interchangeable terms. I use the term value to mean value creation. However, in some cases, an organization is more focused on cost savings than value creation, so in that case, cost is a better term.

The representatives of the departments came back to me with the areas they thought needed improvements in any one of the three categories. What they suggested made sense, and I decided these were the metrics I had been looking for.

QVS also uses the term "speed," which refers to how fast a company is achieving its outputs. So, to recap, QVS measures the quality, value, or speed of the key steps in your process(es) within the scope of the OPTICS exercise.

Now, we can look at each of the key process steps and decide which are the performance opportunities or problem areas we need to improve. But how do we define what those problem areas are? Well, QVS takes us one step closer to creating a prioritized road map for improvement.

QVS is a visual way for you and your team to look at your processes, the people who are impacting those processes, and those impacted by your processes. It then takes the next step and asks what the problems are that exist. It maps out the processes in a clear way so it is easy to see the areas requiring improvement for the whole system to function better.

Metrics and QVS

In some cases, the QVS process is used to simply plug in the already-identified gaps into the matrix. But at this stage, it's possible to start asking if there are certain goals the company would like to achieve around those gaps. For example, going back to the customer service process, one of the gaps was that customer orders were often entered incorrectly.

The number of orders entered incorrectly is a metric that could be incorporated as a goal. For example, how many customer orders are entered in total per month, and how many order entries are inputted incorrectly per month? Perhaps the number of incorrectly input orders is currently seventeen, and the goal is to reduce it to one or zero. That metric can be linked to the core processes.

The QVS process does not always indicate or create metrics. Some QVS data are qualitative rather than quantitative, but there certainly are times when it's possible to incorporate metrics to the SIPOC and QVS in the initial OPTICS meetings, particularly if the data is there.

Case Study

I work with a large general contractor that builds huge industrial park warehouses, hospitals, and schools. Over many years, we have identified over 150 gaps through an iterative OPTICS process conducted with various teams and for various core processes in their organization. As well as identifying 150 gaps, we've also eliminated or dramatically improved on those 150 gaps by aligning the people and processes using the QVS system.

"We have been working with Ryan and his team for several months to identify, align, and document multiple core processes. We knew this was a critical step to effective planning, assigning workload, and training new hires but we really saw the benefits during our sessions with EPS. Ryan has the knowledge and customization that we were looking for!"
—Gina Krusinski, Krusinski Construction

Stage 4 of OPTICS: Building the Accountability Responsibility Matrix (ARM)

The fourth stage of the OPTICS process is building the ARM or the accountability responsibility matrix. After each row is filled out for each key process entry in the SIPOC, the ARM identifies who is accountable for that key process. In other words, the ARM identifies who is responsible for the specific tasks in that row.

It's important to make sure those accountable have what they need to execute the task. This person should understand what they need to do to meet their obligations so the process runs properly. There should only be one accountable person for each row so there is no ambiguity.

In the customer service example, entering a customer order might be one of the tasks or rows. The accountable person for that task or row might be the customer service manager, the customer operations manager, or the director of customer service.

There could even be several people responsible for various tasks. For example, the customer service representative may type in the details of the order into the CRM or ERP system. The salesperson may be responsible for talking to the customer and clarifying anything confusing about the order prior to order entry. However, it's critical that only one person oversees these steps and is held accountable for making sure the order is, ultimately, entered properly.

Frequency

I have claimed the OPTICS system can transform your processes in just six hours by creating the SIPOC strategy map. This is rapid cadence. It's important to note that OPTICS is also an iterative process because your people and processes are constantly changing.

Once you have established an OPTICS system, my recommendation is to have regular OPTICS focus meetings (weekly, monthly, or quarterly) during which you run through the SIPOC process to identify changes, monitor actions, and check on accountability. I also recommend an annual review of the OPTICS strategy map.

The epsoptics.com software platform and mobile app have been developed as an additional tool to enable your team to optimize and align your processes effectively and efficiently.

Case Study

Recalling my client whose company trained hair salon employees, we created the SIPOC, QVS, and ARM within six hours and completely transformed the alignment of responsibility and accountability of their company. As we started to identify the people responsible and accountable for each step of their operations, we uncovered a significant problem.

From the time the company initially made contact with a potential customer to the time when the customer actually received value from the company and began training, that customer was transferred to a different representative four or five times. Customers became confused and frustrated because they didn't know who their contact point was.

During the ARM process when everything was laid out on paper, it became clear why the company was having so many problems. To start with, the customer first spoke with a chat team. The chat team passed the customer on to a salesperson. If the customer qualified as a lead or potential client, they were then passed to the next level of sales and a senior salesperson. If that salesperson determined the customer was ready to sign up, they were passed to someone on the finance team to facilitate payment. Once the payment was made, the finance representative finally passed the customer over to a training coach. At this point, finally, the customer was able to schedule a meeting with a training coach. The problem? It had taken at least five handoffs before the customer saw any value.

You can imagine being a client of this company and being passed from one person to another with no continuity and little personalization. It's not surprising that the customer abandonment rate for the company was off the charts.

What was the answer?

The OPTICS system brought clarity and a solution. Instead of having different people responsible for each step in the sales process, the company decided to use a central concierge. The concierge could facilitate the customer from the initial qualification all the way through to client and coach introductions.

With the introduction of the concierge, instead of four to five handoffs, the client had only one contact before they met their coach and scheduled training. This completely transformed the sales process. The sales employees were no longer pointing fingers at each other and asking why they didn't receive an email or customer data on time.

This one change increased conversions and strengthened the relationship between clients and customers. Customers knew who to contact, and the company's employees were happy to have clarity in their roles and a more efficient system.

It took six hours to transform that business, dramatically increase client retention, and reduce employee frustration. By repurposing the people who were already working on the sales process (the company identified a few of the marketing salespeople who became the concierges), everybody's job became easier.

In short, OPTICS brought clarity around responsibility and accountability.

Stage 5 of OPTICS: The Action Plan

The final stage of OPTICS moves the perspective to the microscopic level. This stage drills down to examine how the various tasks are performed to deliver value to the customer.

Using the customer service process again as an example, I'll explain how this works for entering a customer order into the CRM (customer relationship management) system or ERP (enterprise resource planning) system.

A customer service representative is responsible for entering orders in the system. In the job breakdown, we deconstruct the process into step-by-step instructions for the worker. The job breakdown includes all the tips, tricks, hacks, and safety considerations of the task. Most importantly, the job breakdown outlines **why** each step needs to be done.

This last part is critical and a huge differentiator for OPTICS compared to other systems that document processes. Let me explain why with a case study I like to call "flattening the chicken."

Case Study

Another client I had was a quick-service restaurant chain. The company team and I worked through the OPTICS process and reached the job breakdown stage. We were focusing on ensuring consistency in processes, so we began discussing the specific tasks that the various employees did and the instructions needed in the job breakdowns. One of the restaurant managers looked at me and said, "Ryan, you just don't get it. You know, sometimes we hire new people who don't remember some of the basic tasks. For example, I've got one guy who can't even flatten the chicken consistently."

"All right," I said. "What does flatten the chicken mean? What are you talking about?"

When preparing the chicken, the restaurant manager explained, it was important to flatten it for two reasons. One was that the restaurant made sliders, and if the chicken wasn't flat, the sandwiches were too hard to eat.

"You have to open your mouth really wide," he said.

The second reason was that during the cooking process, if the chicken breast was too thick, it wouldn't cook evenly and could be raw on the inside. Flattening the meat made sure it cooked throughout. Still, no matter how many times the manager told a certain employee to flatten the chicken, he wouldn't do it consistently. According to the manager, he just wasn't capable.

"I must have told him a dozen times," the restaurant manager went on. "He's supposed to flatten the chicken. He's smart enough to know how to flatten the chicken. I give him the meat tenderizer and a piece of chicken and show him, but he just won't do it."

"You said he wasn't capable," I commented. "If I asked that employee *why* he's supposed to flatten the chicken, what would that employee tell me?"

"He would probably look at you like a deer in headlights. He would have no idea why he's supposed to flatten the chicken," the manager responded.

"So, this is a failure in training, not a reflection of the person's capability. You've told me he *has* done it, albeit inconsistently. The problem is he doesn't understand **why** he's supposed to do it—why it's important to do it."

I gave the restaurant manager a homework assignment that day. I told him he should teach the employee the two reasons why he needed to flatten the chicken to the point where the employee understood the reasons and could recite them back to the restaurant manager. In the weeks after, I asked the manager whether the employee was remembering to flatten the chicken.

"Every single time," he said.

I hear managers complain about the younger generations who have been brought up on video games. I hear them claim they aren't capable of doing basic tasks, but the problem is often that the younger generations don't understand the purpose or why the task is important. When they do, they learn and are much more likely to remember to do the task consistently.

The results I repeatedly see with clients show that when people understand the purpose of doing a task, they are more engaged and willing to do it. This goes for process improvements, too. Because if an employee doesn't know why they're doing something, they might take a shortcut.

Employees will often skip steps because they don't understand their importance or may be trying to save time. In more complex environments, those shortcuts can lead to bad results. For example, a shortcut in an order entry process may mean that all the right parts are not on hand to assemble the product a customer needs. This will create a delay in the customer order or even a cancellation of the order.

To summarize, an employee might take a short-cut and decide not to flatten the chicken because they think, "I don't have time to flatten the chicken right now. I don't even know why it's important. I'm just gonna skip it because I've got other stuff to do."

So, the job breakdowns clarify the *how* and, more importantly, the **why** of a task or process.

Employees have access to the OPTICS software. They can see what jobs they are responsible for and access the job breakdown. They can understand the steps they need to take, the *how*, and critically, the *why*, which will motivate them to perform and be accountable for the task.

Workbook: Reader Self-Reflection

Which processes in your organization would benefit most from clearly articulating why they are important?

_____

_____

_____

_____

_____

_____

_____

_____

_____

_____

_____

_____

Key Takeaways

In just six hours, the OPTICS system delivers a road map from the telescopic level down to the microscopic level for operational and process improvements.

The SIPOC breaks down your processes into key steps and clarifies their connection with other steps in your process to facilitate alignment.

The QVS assigns a metric or value to each key task or step to help you understand the value or cost of that step to your overall operations.

The ARM assigns accountability for a task to remove any ambiguity.

The job breakdowns explain how the task is done, including the how and, critically, the why.

The action plan created during OPTICS enables your team to close gaps, solve problems, and hold people accountable.

4

How the Customer Journey Parallels Your Operations and Why That Matters

I mentioned before that OPTICS applies to both internal and external processes. However, fundamentally, OPTICS is about the customer journey and aligning your processes with that journey.

I first started to develop the OPTICS concept over ten-plus years ago. When I looked at the way I was approaching internal process improvements, I realized that if we reviewed the customer journey first and understood that process, we could take those insights and use them to better align internal processes.

When companies seek operational improvements—efficiencies to be cheaper, faster, or whatever metric they consider important—the first place they tend to look is at their internal processes. The problem with that approach, however, is if you change something internally to increase speed or reduce cost, it can hurt your customer journey or damage one of your other processes later.

A company can find itself in a cycle where, despite making changes, they are not improving their internal processes, and the changes are increasing, not decreasing, customer dissatisfaction. For example, a shortcut taken in the beginning of a process might create a bigger problem further down the line. A SIPOC would show how that shortcut would affect the rest of the process and if it should be implemented or not.

This chapter applies a similar process as the SIPOC-building to create alignment between the customer journey and the associated internal and external processes.

In the previous chapter, we introduced the training company with excessive customer handoffs or touchpoints early in the customer journey. These handoffs were causing frustration among the sales team and causing customers to rethink their relationship with the company.

In this case, instead of looking at the internal processes of the training company, we began by first mapping the customer journey. For example, we asked: How does the customer find out about the company? How does the customer first interact with the sales team? How does the company convert leads to customers? How and when does the customer begin to receive value from the company? How does the company retain customers and continue to provide them with value? By finding the answers to these questions, we can build a SIPOC and map out the customer journey.

What is the significance of the customer journey? From my experience, if your internal operations parallel your customer journey, that's when your customer receives maximum value. When your internal operations are aligned with your customer journey, your processes and systems run smoothly and optimally. There is minimal confusion among internal teams, and customers are led through a logical and hopefully seamless process from initial contact to payment and the receipt of goods and services.

Creating a SIPOC from the perspective of the customer journey maps out your internal operations and identifies what is causing frustration. It could be that excessive handoffs between departments or between people in departments are a source of stress for your team and your customers.

When a customer is not taken care of, receives a wrong shipment, or drops out, the problem escalates within the organization. An employee might point the finger at another employee or department and accuse them of not doing their job correctly. These types of issues often create chaos.

The SIPOC process outlines the steps in the customer journey so the teams involved can identify the key pain points customers are experiencing. Ironically, they are often the same pain points the employees are experiencing.

Case Study

The significance of aligning the customer journey with internal processes was clear when I introduced OPTICS to a plastics manufacturing company. When we prepared the SIPOC from the customer journey perspective, we asked similar questions of the company: How do your customers find out about you? How do they become customers? How do you create value for the customer? How do you nurture your customer relationships?

The inputs we found were interesting. For example, we found that the initial customer quotation sales order needed to flow through the entire process. Not only did the sales team need access to the information, but the pricing and customer service teams did, too. Also, the engineering team needed to see the quote because they had to draw the plans to execute on the quote provided to the customer. Finally, the production team needed access to the quote so they could add it to their deliverables.

In the first few meetings, as we created the SIPOC or customer journey map, it became clear how many different players needed access to the initial quote. Because of this, the company began reenvisioning their CRM system so each of the different departments had access. This process explained why different actors were always going back and forth with the sales team, engineering, customer service, or other parties to get access to the quote and why the processes were hampered.

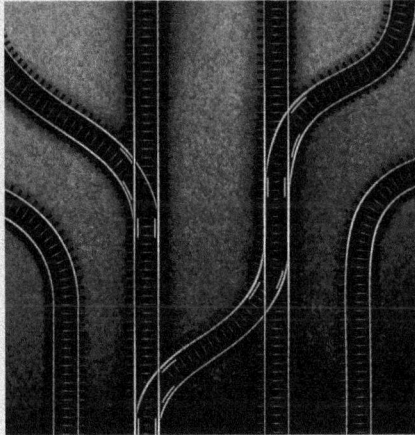

This case study shows that OPTICS applies to both internal and external people and processes. It is a three-dimensional, cross-functional tool to bring clarity and break down silos between departments.

The starting point for OPTICS for many firms is to deconstruct their customer journey map. We can then identify the key internal operations that need to be matched up with the customer journey. Think of the customer journey and internal processes as two trains on dual parallel rails that link up.

I often find when working with companies that their sales and operations teams see processes through different lenses. Sales and marketing teams see processes as a hindrance to business. Sales and marketing people are creatives who don't like to be bound by systems and processes. Operations teams, however, consider processes the lifeblood of what they do and how they do things. For operations, systems and processes keep projects running according to deadlines and delivery dates.

The reason the customer journey and internal processes are on parallel paths is because there is usually a sales and marketing effort for a prospective customer to find you. A CRM tool creates forecasts depending on whether a customer comes on board, and the supply chain adapts as it plans for the new orders. While the salesperson is forecasting when someone may become a client, there's a parallel operations process that plans for the production process and delivery of the service or product. So, sales and operations run in parallel.

The customer service team needs to communicate with the supply chain and production team to inform them when an order has been received. The production team needs to report back on how quickly the production team can fill the order. That lead time will impact whether the order is finalized and completed.

Thus, at each step in the customer journey, there's a parallel operational process. The customer places the order and receives confirmation when the order has been received. Meanwhile, the operations team is scaling up to produce the order, whether it's a service, product, or rental. Now, we reach the core operations of value delivery, and the final step is converting that one-time customer into a repeat customer.

Both the customer service team and operations are involved in making sure the customer is being contacted regularly to see if they have another order and their needs are met. These steps boost customer retention and are opportunities to upsell and intro duce other products or services.

Sometimes, sales and marketing teams rebel against processes. As a result, they fail to pass critical information to the operations team which cannot service the customer and the customer service team.

I think you would agree this situation is a crazy cycle of dysfunction. If the sales team does not pass the information to the operations team that it needs to meet orders efficiently, then neither team can support the other and serve the customer.

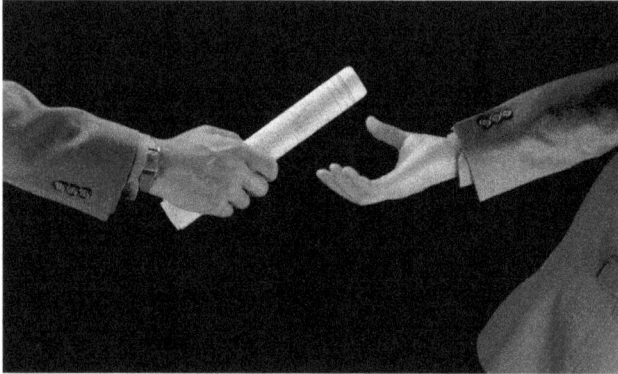

The main takeaway here is that when people think about processes, I would estimate that 95 percent of the time, they immediately think of operations to the exclusion of all else. When I mention that I help organizations align people in processes to accelerate performance, the response I get back is, "Oh, so you mean the operations or manufacturing."

I always need to bring them back to their clients' journey, sales processes, human resources, and operations. Every one of these groups has a process that needs to be aligned.

As I mentioned earlier, if the operations teams are the only ones focusing on internal processes, they often fail to address the external needs of the process, the most important of which is the needs of the customer. This causes the salesperson to become frustrated, and in turn, the operations team becomes frustrated.

If the focus is first on the sales or the customer journey map, you can engage the sales team, which will enable your operations team to identify the areas that need significant improvement.

The Voice of the Customer Process, VOCP

Central to the customer journey is the concept of the voice of the customer. I first learned about this concept in the early 2000s and trademarked the voice of the customer process (VOCP) in 2006. There are three components to the concept: VOC (voice of the customer), VOP (voice of the process), and VOCP (voice of the customer process).

- **VOC** = Voice of the customer: listen to the customer
- **VOP** = Voice of the process: look at internal operations processes and statistical analysis
- **VOCP** = Voice of the customer process: what can I learn from observing my customer's process that will enhance my internal capabilities to create value for them?

- **VOC = Voice of the customer: listen to the customer**

- **VOP = Voice of the process: look at internal operations processes and statistical analysis**

- **VOCP = Voice of the customer process: what can I learn from observing my customer's process that will enhance my internal capabilities to create value for them?**

Voice of the Customer (VOC)

The voice of the customer is often shortened to VOC. It is an idea or way for companies to gather customer data. For example, companies often arrange focus groups to listen to their customers and gather feedback on their products and services. They collect surveys and conduct beta testing to understand the customer experiences with their brand and to make sure they're offering products the customer wants.

The Voice of the Process (VOP)

The voice of the process is an internal process. Companies typically collect and examine data on their production or operational processes to measure performance. For example, they might track the number of defective products in a batch, labor efficiency, or the number of products produced per month. These types of metrics are the VOP.

Now, do you see the conflict between the VOC and the VOP? The VOC is looking at what the customer wants, but the VOP is looking at internal operations and performance efficiencies. The two are apples and oranges and cannot be examined together for correlations.

It's interesting to get survey feedback from a customer who asks, "That's valuable information; now, what do we do with it?" And it's interesting to look at a process and ask, "That's valuable information; now, how can we get more efficient?" The answer to these questions lies in aligning customer needs and the operational process. In other words, we can observe the customer process and then consider how the internal processes can change to better serve everyone involved.

The Voice of the Customer Process (VOCP)

One of the most fascinating stories I've ever heard in consumer products involved the Proctor and Gamble air freshener product Febreze. When this product was first launched, it struggled to gain traction in the market. Proctor and Gamble used a VOC approach and asked consumers for feedback on the Febreze product. Using that data, the company delivered what they heard the customer asking for—a scientifically developed product that eliminated odor particles from the air. The internal data showed just how effective their product was at eliminating odors, and the external VOC data showed that this was what the consumer wanted. Still, customers did not buy the product on a repeat basis. Why?

One reason was that people become inured to the odors in their own homes. So, because they tended not to smell odors in their homes, there was no trigger to cause them to buy Febreze. The company then decided to observe consumers using Febreze in their homes to see if that would yield insights as to how to better market the product as a cleaning product.

When they watched consumers clean their homes, they noticed they didn't use the product at the beginning of the cleaning process to eliminate odors as expected. What they did notice was a consistent habit of fluffing cushions when the person had finished cleaning. As they fluffed, consumers smiled, implying satisfaction and contentment.

This gave Proctor and Gamble the idea of marketing Febreze as the finishing touch on a job well done and a key component of the satisfaction experienced by consumers when they finish cleaning their homes. This marketing strategy using VOCP and not just the VOC worked! Sales skyrocketed.

This story illustrates how customers often can't clearly communicate what they want from a product or service, so relying solely on VOC is a bad idea.

When I first heard this story, I realized that if you are only asking your customers for feedback or you're only asking your internal operations people to improve their processes, you're missing the point of how you could transform your business when you observe your customer's process. If you do both and use VOCP, you can build a framework for improving your internal operations based on your customer experience.

Would You Like to Own a Purple Car?

Recently, I have spoken at a number of forums about the customer experience (CX). Mark Nicholson is the founder and facilitator of CX Forums. I led the forum in Chicago in 2022 and learned many other anecdotes confirming the value of VOCP. The purple car is another particular favorite.

Would you like to own a purple car? The reality is that many people will say they would consider owning a purple car. However, when you look at the VOCP, hardly anybody owns or has owned a purple car. Except me.

Years ago, I was in sales and received my first company car. I selected the car online and picked out the features I wanted. One of the features I could select was the color of the interior and exterior. I viewed the external colors online and was taken by a dark red hue called "merlot," which I thought sounded super sophisticated. I selected my merlot sports model. Some days later, what showed up in my driveway was a bit of a shock. Those dark red hues were more like a crayon purple. I thought, *This is a purple car, right?*

In this case, VOC had been dead wrong. What I thought I wanted wasn't at all what I really wanted.

Another example I like to use to illustrate the value of VOCP is Bluetooth technology. If a company had asked people in the early 2000s what features they would like to see in their cars, few people would have said the ability to talk to their car and have it dial their spouse, business colleague, or whomever hands-free because they would never have envisaged it as a possibility.

People did not foresee Bluetooth technology, and it would not have materialized from VOC. A certain color of car, type of interior, or gas mileage might have, but an innovation like Bluetooth would only have emerged with VOCP.

Bluetooth was a result of the increasing use of mobile phones in the early to mid-2000s and the increasing number of accidents caused by distracted drivers using their phones. When drivers were observed, It became obvious that a technological breakthrough was needed to improve the safety of cars and give customers what they needed and wanted from their cars.

To sum up, VOCP can fuel innovation, improve your internal employee communications, and simplify how they hand off processes between departments. Ultimately, VOCP, as a component of OPTICS, helps your internal employees, leadership team, and customers by getting everybody on the same page. This is accomplished with the customer journey map linking customer needs and internal operations. In other words, OPTICS aligns your customer sales and operations teams on a clear, mutually beneficial path to success.

Workbook: Reader Self-Reflection

What misalignments exist between the journey your customer takes and the internal processes in your business?

_____

_____

_____

_____

Key Takeaways

- OPTICS is about aligning the journey your customer takes with your internal business processes for better results.

- Your customer receives maximum value when your internal operations parallel the journey your customer takes.

- The SIPOC process outlines the steps in the customer journey to identify the key pain points customers are experiencing. Ironically, they are often the same pain points the employees are experiencing.

- VOC is not sufficient to serve customers. VOCP, as a component of OPTICS, aligns your customer sales and operations teams on a mutually beneficial path to success.

5

The Evolution of OPTICS

"My core belief is that clearly aligned processes allow your team to perform, create value, and ultimately fulfill your organization's purpose. Our team's goal is to help your company clarify, simplify, and align processes through an organized system enthusiastically documented and followed by all."
—Ryan Weiss

OPTICS was born out of application, not just theory. I have applied all the elements of OPTICS in my work with companies and teams of all sizes, from startups to multinationals. Finally, OPTICS is not just a process; it has evolved into a software platform to help teams and organizations align and execute better by solving their problems.

There are many other process documentation software stacks and applications. Many of them solve different problems, and some simply capture processes in a semi-organized way, but as I explain the evolution of OPTICS, its exceptional value-add will become clear.

The OPTICS Story

Early in my corporate career, I found that just solving various parts of a process in a vacuum really didn't account for all the other variables affecting the process. It might solve one particular issue in one part of the supply chain or production line, but it did not compel the sought-after improvements and could even cause more disruption further down the line.

The SIPOC

Early process documentation software just looked at processes through the lens of operational steps, not through the eyes of the people executing the process. At this time, I was quite the introvert, a nerd with degrees in chemistry and finance. However, when I worked with clients, I was interested in the relationship between their systems and the people who controlled them. The company I was working for at the time sent me to Dale Carnegie training—Dale Carnegie is the acclaimed author of the book, *How to Win Friends and Influence People*—to help me with my interactions and be more effective with clients.

This training taught me that excellent communicators don't talk about themselves; they talk to others about what's important to them. They ask questions and learn about the other person rather than focusing on what they want to share about themselves.

Around the same time I took the Dale Carnegie training, I trained in Lean Six Sigma, another process improvement approach that introduced me to a tool called the SIPOC. With Lean Six Sigma, the SIPOC integrates internal processes with the suppliers, inputs, process outputs, and customers. It focuses on a specific internal process, such as a manufacturing or accounting process, and looks for ways to make these internal processes more efficient or productive.

Using my new communication skills from Dale Carnegie and the SIPOC approach, I made an accidental connection between a tool for internal teams and the concept of developing relationships with external people or external teams.

I applied the SIPOC to clients' processes to frame out the steps of their processes, to identify the customers of their processes, what the customers need from the process, the outputs of the process, the inputs required by the process to create the outputs that the customers care about, and the suppliers of the inputs.

That all sounds very complicated, but asking these questions revealed what the client was all about. Getting the answers gave me almost magical insights from which the client and I could develop a framework together for improvements. I did this for a piano teacher, a banker, a librarian, a large manufacturing company, and a diaper manufacturer. I even began to look at my own processes in this way as I started to realize how universal this tool was in exploring the relationships between people and processes and the different types of organizations—banks, manufacturing, and services or rental agencies.

Each time I started down the journey of asking people questions, we would sketch out a framework, or a SIPOC, on a simple sheet of paper. At the end of the conversation, the client would pick up the piece of paper and ask, "I can keep this, right?" I had stumbled onto an incredibly powerful tool that was providing insights into people's processes and giving them clarity as to how their teams could improve the processes.

Quality, Value, Speed (QVS)

The second piece of OPTICS to evolve was the QVS: quality, value, speed. I first used this with a team I was managing in the Philippines approximately ten years ago. My team suddenly grew from a few people to hundreds of people, and I needed a common framework to look at all of the teams in a very simple way to see how their processes were performing. I was looking for components or metrics to measure their performance.

I identified quality, cost, and timeliness as the three components and looked at what insights the teams could give me about the quality, cost, and timeliness of their processes.

For any process, you can define a certain level of quality. Some processes demand an extremely high level of quality. For other processes, it's not so important. Regarding cost, every process has a value associated with it. For example, it could be outstanding receivables, a revenue value for a sales process, or gross profit. Finally, for timeliness, there is some time or speed component to every process.

With these metrics, I created a simple matrix and posted it outside my office. I asked each team to develop a *quality* metric that they wanted to improve, a *value* metric that they wanted to improve, and a *speed or timeliness* metric they wanted to improve—three metrics per team.

The QVS developed into an experimental tool whereby the teams would look at their quality, value, or speed, and try different ways to make improvements wherever needed. I then linked the SIPOC with the QVS metrics.

Accountability Responsibility Matrix (ARM)

The SIPOC and QVS pinpointed possible changes in team behavior that would lead to process results, but the problem was how to ensure those behaviors occurred. That's when I developed the RA matrix. This step in the approach identified who is accountable and who is responsible for different activities in a department. What these people were exactly responsible for had to be identified.

The responsible party is the person who does the action or documents an action, such as turning a valve or sending out a calendar invite. To be accountable is to be the person "where the buck stops." This is the supervisor or person with some higher level of authority than the person who is responsible. This person is accountable for making sure the tasks are done by the responsible person, or they can delegate the task to someone else. The ARM is holding people accountable for their responsibilities and monitoring that accountability.

Next, I learned about a theory called stakeholder analysis. At this point in my career, I was driving a lot to meet with different clients. On one particular trip, I was driving from Kansas City to Indianapolis, and I was listening to a book on tape about the American Revolutionary War. The book examined what compels people into war, and the topic moved to stakeholder analysis.

In elementary school, we learn that America fought for its independence because of taxation without representation. American colonists were frustrated because they were paying taxes to the British, but they had no voice in how they were being taxed or how the taxes were used. On the other hand, the British had every right to be taxing the American colonists because they were sending resources, such as soldiers and weapons, to protect them during the French and Indian War from 1754 to 1763. With Britain's resources, primarily the slaves, the American colonies were becoming productive and efficient.

The British implemented a stamp tax, tea tax, and molasses tax. That last tax really hit hard because it affected rum and alcohol consumption. Getting upset about a molasses tax made no sense to me as a child, but as an adult who enjoys an occasional rum, I can completely understand it now.

The takeaway here is that conducting a stakeholder analysis shows you who is vested in the process and what their roles are. Clearly, a failure to understand these dynamics has led to war, and not just the American Revolutionary War. Virtually every war has some element of stakeholder disenfranchisement.

Job Breakdown

By the time I linked these three elements, I had spent twenty years developing my ideas, and I thought I had made great strides in documentation and aligning people and processes. But then, a client in the chemical industry asked me if I could modernize Training Within Industry (TWI).

I had no idea what TWI was, so I looked it up. It was a series of training programs developed during World War II that enables US companies to hire and train huge numbers of new workers to replace those who had gone to war. It was a seventy- or eighty-year-old system, but I wondered why it was relevant.

As I researched TWI, I learned about the job breakdown, which is a simple tool that answers questions about what needs to be done, how it should be done, and why it is important. In my twenty years of working on procedures and documentation, I had never seen a tool with such a simple yet invaluable purpose. This became a new component I added to my existing frameworks.

The job breakdown, however, is highly detailed. It is not done at the organizational or departmental level; it's done at the individual task level. It's a work instruction for a task or a standard operating procedure. Think flattening the chicken.

Ultimately, I put all the different components together: the SIPOC, the QVS, the ARM framework, and the job breakdown. And that was the birth of OPTICS.

OPTICS Today

More recently, I attended a conference called The Purpose Summit. The concept centered on an organization's purpose—why an organization does what it does. During the conference, I started building out the front end of the OPTICS system: its purpose, the why of the system, the scope, and the gaps it closes.

To conclude the evolution of OPTICS, it is the system that propels your organization into the future. It is aligning people and processes to accelerate performance. The better aligned your people and processes are, the stronger your propulsion and the stronger the acceleration will be for your organization.

This brings me to the P5 Rocket, a concept I came up with before I developed OPTICS. The P5 Rocket was the precursor to OPTICS and helps me to explain why OPTICS works.

Workbook: Reader Self-Reflection

Question 1. How would better definitions of quality, value, and speed improve the outcomes of your business?

_____

_____

_____

_____

_____

Question 2. How would greater clarity of accountability and responsibility improve the outcomes of your business?

_____

_____

_____

_____

_____

Key Takeaways

The value-added by the OPTICS system has been proven in hundreds of cases.

OPTICS evolved over time, integrating philosophies such as Dale Carnegie's approach to relationships, Lean Six Sigma, and stakeholder theory.

OPTICS is more than an evolved theory; it is a practical tool and software to align teams and processes to propel your organization into the future.

6

OPTICS and the P5 Rocket

"Would you tell me, please, which way I ought to go from here?"

"That depends a good deal on where you want to get to," said the Cat.

"I don't much care where—" said Alice.

"Then it doesn't matter which way you go," said the Cat.

—Lewis Carroll, Alice in Wonderland

The P5 Rocket theory was the precursor to OPTICS. I explore it in detail in my first book, *From Orangutan to Rocket Scientist: How to Lead and Engage Your Team Through an Effective Process.*

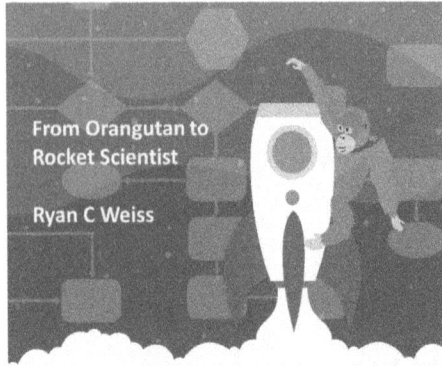

From Orangutan to
Rocket Scientist

Ryan C Weiss

How to Lead & Engage Your Team with Effective Process!

The book describes the P5 Rocket as the propulsion for your strategic plan. When I developed OPTICS, I saw it as the operating system that makes sure the rocket functions optimally. Here's P5 Rocket theory in a nutshell and how OPTICS integrates with that theory.

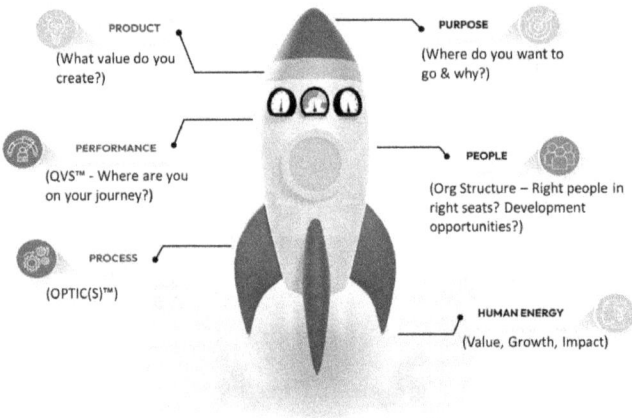

PRODUCT
(What value do you create?)

PURPOSE
(Where do you want to go & why?)

PERFORMANCE
(QVS™ - Where are you on your journey?)

PEOPLE
(Org Structure – Right people in right seats? Development opportunities?)

PROCESS
(OPTIC(S)™)

HUMAN ENERGY
(Value, Growth, Impact)

P5 Rocket Theory

The P5 Rocket represents your organization, and it has six components to it: the 5Ps—Purpose, Product, Performance, People, and Process—and Propulsion.

Each of the Ps are critical components of an organization, and OPTICS is the operating and support system ensuring they work together for lift-off, acceleration, and optimal functioning.

P1 – Purpose

The nose cone of the rocket represents your organization's purpose. If the nose cone of the rocket is pointed in the wrong direction, your organization is going to go in the wrong direction. But it's more involved than that. If you point your rocket toward the moon, you won't land on the moon. Traveling to the moon requires navigating and making calculated course corrections along the way. If your nose cone is just a millimeter off when you leave Earth, by the time you get to the moon, you will be off by thousands of miles.

P2 – Product

The second component of the rocket is the product, which is how the organization creates value for its customers. Consider it the payload. This is the material the rocket or organization is carrying that is creating value for the stakeholders and customers. Dr. John King is a rocket scientist, astronaut, thought leader, and motivational speaker. In an interview, he told me about some of his work with NASA as an astronaut. He shared with me that back in the early days of space exploration, they had to learn how to fit ten pounds of software in a five-pound box. That was the payload for their mission. In terms of your organization, is the payload a product, service, or something else? How are you creating value for your customers?

P3 – Performance

The third component is performance. Performance is measured by the strength of the thrust or impulsion of your rocket. There are so many factors that influence performance. In a rocket ship, the astronauts need to track their current location, monitor their direction, and calculate their future path. Ground control monitors the heart rates of the astronauts, their health, and mental state. Similarly, an organization has to monitor its employees and its systems and think just as holistically.

The QVS component of OPTICS applies here. The rocket ship concept illustrates why QVS is critical. If you look at performance only in terms of speed or how fast you are moving, other things can fall apart. If the rocket travels too fast, the tiles on the rocket ship might become damaged. If the astronauts are burned out, the quality of their work suffers, and they might make mistakes in calculations.

Similarly, if an organization only focuses on cutting costs to increase profit, other factors suffer, such as worker morale and the quality of the product. At the other extreme, if you only focus on quality and producing the most premium product on the market, you will price yourself out of the market.

The right balance must be established between quality, value, and speed. Quality has to have a value component so that the price includes the right margin to cover costs and suit the market. There also has to be a timeliness component to each process. If you can only produce one part per day, you'll need a high profit margin for each unit because if the quality is bad, it will take you a whole day to make another one. If you have high-volume production, you can have a low-cost margin for each unit. Thus, you can follow different strategies based on your product mix or your service mix.

P4 – People

The fourth component of the rocket is your people. Do you have the right ground crew and leaders to make sure your mission is successful? In your organization, do you have the right people in the right seats on your leadership team? Also, what's the level of engagement of those people? Are they excited? Are they working together and collaborative? Are you recruiting the right people? Are you monitoring their mental and physical health? Are you supporting them and helping them grow? Are they creating value?

You can't just measure people based on productivity; they are not machines. If you do that, your team will burn out or leave, and you'll find it difficult to compete in the labor market. Today, the human aspect of work culture is front and center in the minds of the millennial and Gen Z populations. Younger generations want to work for organizations with a positive social impact, not those focused solely on profit.

P5 – Process

The last of the five Ps is your process. The bottom of a rocket has directional fins to adjust the direction of the rocket ship. The thrusters move in different directions to adjust the speed and direction of the rocket. For the thrusters to do their job effectively, all the Ps have to align and function optimally. If departments do not coordinate or if systems have bottlenecks, performance is stymied, value is lost, and the mission fails.

I often say that people without processes become frustrated and processes without people are wasted. And in strategy sessions, there is always debate about where the focus should be. Is it more important to focus on *who* does things, or is it more important to focus on *how* you do things?

The reality is that you should focus on both at the same time.

I often ask business leaders what happens if they hire the ideal candidate—the person who can transform their business—but there is a problem because their processes are broken. The answer every time is that the person will become frustrated, disengaged, and quit. You can hire the best person, but bad processes will chew them up and spit them out. To quote Dr. W. Edwards Deming, "A bad system will beat a good person every time."

That's true about your best customers, your best employees, and your best vendors. So, creating good systems to enable people to perform, create value, and fulfill your organization's purpose is what the P5 Rocket is all about.

Propulsion (Human Energy)

The final element is the fuel and propulsion that your rocket needs to launch, accelerate, and make progress on its journey. In an organization, this is human energy and financial capital. Maximum human energy is generated when employees are healthy and happy, and financial capital needs to be generated through successful operations to continue operations.

I have worked with startups that have used the P5 model to create their business plan. Initially, startups have no launch pad and no revenues. They just have a vision. If they follow the P5 model, they can build a business plan by asking the following questions:

1. What's the **purpose** of my company?
2. What **product** am I going to sell, and how am I going to sell it?
3. What's my strategy, and how am I going to measure **performance**?
4. What **people** do I need on my team to be successful in starting up, and what support do they need?
5. What **processes** do I need to get in place to launch?

Many startups fail to launch because they lack initial combustion or propulsion. Startups need access to capital. They need loans or financing that will provide the fuel for initial launch, but the startup needs to also generate cashflow to sustain the momentum and propulsion. A rocket might reach the moon, but it won't venture into another solar system without additional fuel. So, a company has to find a way to generate additional capital as it operates.

The "great resignation" was a prominent discussion early in 2023 when employee engagement was at an all-time low. This was a bad omen for the long-term sustainability of organizations. A startup or company might have plenty of capital or fuel to start with, but at some point, they run out of human energy, and financial capital won't fix the problem unless your employees are engaged and your systems and processes align.

Workbook: Reader Self-Reflection

How would better alignment of the 5Ps propel your business to new heights?

_____

_____

_____

_____

_____

_____

_____

_____

_____

_____

Key Takeaways

- **OPTICS is the operating system for your P5 Rocket (organization).**

- **The 5Ps are purpose, product, performance, people, and process. All five need to align.**

- **With the addition of human energy and financial capital (propulsion), you have lift-off and acceleration.**

Now that you can see what OPTICS can do for your people and processes, ***are you ready to launch?***

Check out the VR P5 Rocket experience at
www.p5rocket.com.

7

Executing OPTICS

People often ask me, "Where should I start? Should I start with the P5 Rocket, or should I start with OPTICS?" My answer is both. Your organization is the rocket, but your rocket won't go anywhere without a system to operate it, and that system is OPTICS. OPTICS is the people and the processes working together, which translates into the habits, behaviors, and reliance that people have on the processes.

Human Behavior and OPTICS

There are many examples of how the relationship between people and processes can be detrimental to an organization if ill-managed. For example, if people don't believe a process works or they don't understand the purpose behind a process or task, they will take shortcuts. Recall flattening the chicken.

People also have to trust systems or processes. If astronauts have reason to doubt their rocket systems, they'll do what they think will get the job done best, perhaps sabotaging the mission.

Interpersonal relations are critical too. You could have the best processes, but if people don't trust each other or the politics are toxic, there will be infighting, and the mission will not succeed.

In rocket science, maximum dynamic pressure, or max Q, is the moment in the launch when the rocket experiences "maximum mechanical stress." The rocket is subjected to extreme physical pressure as it travels at high speed through the atmosphere. In fact, this is the greatest point of stress during the entire launch, and even a minuscule amount of additional pressure could cause systems to fail and the rocket to explode.

I believe a similar thing happens in organizations. If you put too much pressure on the people and the systems, the process will fail. On the other hand, if you don't put sufficient pressure on the team and the processes and people don't understand the vision or the reason behind the processes, they disengage, and the systems also fail. So, managing or monitoring the processes and the pressure in the organization is an essential part of change management.

Stuck Street

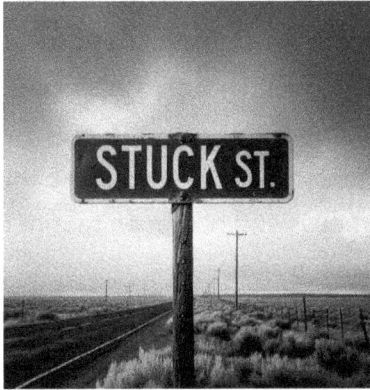

At a conference I went to, a speaker told a story about a squirrel on Stuck Street. We have all driven down a street and seen a squirrel in the road running back and forth because it can't decide which way to go. If we don't slow down, the squirrel is going to be stuck in Stuck Street, or worse, flattened.

The analogy here is that companies can choose which way to go regarding alignment. You can choose to focus on people, or you can focus on processes, but the best option is to align those two things so you're going in one direction. If your people and process are misaligned, then you'll find yourself on Stuck Street.

I worked in the chemical industry for a while. When I worked in my first manufacturing plant, a young man was in charge of receiving. He regularly received a huge bulk tank truck with 40,000 pounds of chemicals. This young man had been taught not to test the quality of the material when it came in, just to assume it was correct, and to write down a number on the quality control checklist so he could then pump the material into the bulk tank. Because he did not understand the reasoning behind the quality control process and had been taught not to worry about it, he took a shortcut.

About a year after I arrived at the plant, the tank truck came in, the receiver connected it up to a bulk tank, and pumped the material into the tank. As he had been trained, he went into the lab, wrote down the number, and went about his day.

Somebody realized the wrong material had been pumped into the wrong tank. The reason for the quality control test was not just because they needed to test the quality of the material; it was also to double-check that the right material was being pumped into the right tank. We had 40,000 pounds of chemical in the wrong tank. We had to pump it out, clean it out, dispose of the material properly, and do other costly procedures because the process and the person were not aligned. The shortcut the receiver took based on how he was trained left us stuck on Stuck Street.

By the way, the receiver in this case was a valued employee; he had just been improperly trained because there was a misalignment between the people and the process. This wasn't a people problem at the operator level—it was a system problem.

The First Six Hours

I claimed in Chapter 3 that OPTICS can transform a business in six hours. It's a lofty claim, so let me walk you through the initial hours of OPTICS and you can see for yourself what the early execution looks like.

Bear in mind the goal is to use OPTICS as a support mechanism over the long term. As business owners, you know nothing stands still, so the first six hours are the beginning of an ongoing transformation. That said, within that time frame, I guarantee you will see movement and the foundations for longer-term growth and sustainability in your business operations.

In six hours, OPTICS delivers a road map that will begin to lay out what the next three to five years could look like and how your business could be different. Here's how.

Preparation for the OPTICS Workshop

I have introduced the OPTICS system hundreds of times for core processes with various clients. I always begin with an initial six-hour workshop. In those six hours, we discuss the company initially from a ten-thousand-foot perspective and work through the OPTICS system. We create job breakdowns, brainstorm suggestions on how to close gaps, resolve issues, and conclude with the document approval process.

As a reminder, OPTICS is a system to align people and processes to accelerate performance. It can be done at a high strategic level—a single OPTICS for the whole organization—or it can be done at a finer level for an operations department, an admin department, or any process or component of your operations. So, the very first step is to define what process we are focusing on. In other words, we define the scope of OPTICS.

Step 1: Overview — Defining the Purpose, Scope, and Gaps

Purpose:
It is critical to efficiently provide first aid to our employees when an incident occurs. It is also essential to follow the proper protocol in order to ensure corrective actions are put in place to prevent future injuries & minimize cost / insurance impact.

Scope Start:
Starts when an incident occurs

Scope End:
Completed when corrective actions are put in place to minimize future potential incidents

Gaps:
- 1 incident last year – Goal is ZERO
- Past employee was sent to wrong urgent care!
- Insurance company informed us we need to improve process

Some preparation is required in advance of the first six hours. Determining the scope of the exercise ensures that the right people are in the room when we start OPTICS.

For example, if we are focusing on the operations department and only have salespeople in the room, we're not going to get the buy-in of the operations people. If we are focusing on a process in Chicago and only have people from Boston, it's a problem. So, some technical details need to be ironed out before the first six hours.

Defining the Purpose

The next detail to solidify is the purpose of the process. The preceding screenshot shows the initial OPTICS data input process. This example is for a manufacturing company attempting to improve the investigative processes for workers' compensation after an injury. Health and safety protocols are critical for the workplace. They help companies avoid accidents and expensive litigation and preserve their reputation as a stellar employer who cares about their employees. The purpose of this particular OPTICS was to ensure first aid is provided efficiently when an accident occurs and the right protocols are followed.

Defining the Scope

The scope in the example OPTICS exercise is based on a timeline. That timeline is from the moment an accident happens to the time corrective actions are taken in the process and system to prevent injuries and accidents from occurring.

In other words, this OPTICS exercise is going to examine what happens system-wise and people-wise when an accident occurs. When is first aid administered? Who administers it? What is the process for calling emergency services? Who makes the decision to call emergency services? What is the decision based on? What paperwork is filled out and filed after an incident? Who is responsible for the paperwork? What steps need to be taken to improve safety in the organization? Is the workplace OSHA compliant? Is there a health and safety handbook? And so on.

Defining the Gaps

Gaps:
- 1 incident last year – Goal is ZERO
- Past employee was sent to wrong urgent care!
- Insurance company informed us we need to improve process

The screenshot shows the identified gaps that need to be resolved. These gaps are known from the very beginning, but gaps will also be revealed during the road map–building process.

In the example shown, one employee was sent to the wrong urgent care facility. This could have cost the company undue medical expenses, so finding out why it happened and instituting changes to prevent it from happening again will close that gap.

Another identified gap is that the insurance company was requesting a more thorough investigative process with better documentation to process any claims. So, updating and improving the accident protocols and reporting processes will close that gap.

These steps are all done in preparation for the first session, and they are designed to establish the following:

1. What process(es) is OPTICS focusing on? **(SCOPE)**
2. Why is this our focus? **(PURPOSE)**
3. What gaps are we hoping to close when we go through the OPTICS process? **(GAPS)**

With these three questions answered, we can determine who should participate in the workshop and help build out the SIPOC.

**OPTICS is
a system to
align people
and processes
to accelerate
performance.**

Step 2. The First Meeting: Building the SIPOC

My initial meeting with a client group includes an introduction to OPTICS. I am never surprised to hear that most clients don't know what OPTICS is. I am often asked how OPTICS differs from the P5 Rocket or if it is the same thing. So we all need to align on what OPTICS is and why we are doing OPTICS before we turn our attention to the company itself and building the SIPOC.

Suppliers	Inputs	Process	Outputs	Customers
Employee	Injury	Incident Occurs	Injury Notify Manager on Duty	MOD Employees
MOD	Significant injury? Small cut, bruise, injured finger, etc.	Determine if it may be life-threatening or urgent care	If life-threatening or if there is any doubt, call 911. If urgent care only, then call Nurses hotline.	911 Nurses Hotline
MOD HR	Phone call Employee Information (Maria to create & update file)	Call Nurses Hotline 888-333-3334 Review annually to confirm no changes	Reference Number Phone Number NH Notifies Work Comp Insurance Company	Nurses Hotline Insurance Company MOD / Affected Employee
Nurses Hotline	Reference Number Phone Number	Share reference number & phone number with affected employee	Inform employee to call	Employee

The first step in building the SIPOC is to start identifying the key process steps. For the moment, forget the inputs and outputs, suppliers, and customers that you see in the above example. We'll get to those.

We have already established that the scope of this process starts when an incident occurs and ends when corrective actions are put into place to minimize potential future incidents. So, the key process steps for the SIPOC begin when the incident occurs. After that, the next action is to determine whether an injury is life-threatening or can be handled by urgent care, then to call the nurse hotline, which should be updated each year and a note added to that effect.

The updating of the nurse's hotline number may seem like a low-priority item. But it is actually a critical item. Consider that flight attendants on commercial planes have a phone with a hotline they use to contact medical services on the ground anytime there's a medical incident on the plane. The medical providers change from year to year, but imagine if a flight attendant had the wrong hotline number and there was an emergency on the plane. A situation could go from bad to worse. It's vital, then, that everybody can access the right number. And that's true for airlines and any manufacturing company.

During the meeting, the team reviews and records the process steps in detail from start to finish in the SIPOC in the OPTICS software. Note that the scope can always be abbreviated or extended. The beauty of OPTICS is its versatility and ability to bring clarity and purpose to complex systems and processes.

After an incident has occurred, the manager on duty determines whether the injury is life-threatening or can be treated by urgent care. If there is any doubt about whether the injury is serious, the protocol is to call 911. That is the number one priority.

If the injury is considered less serious and can be treated by urgent care, the protocol is to call the nurse's hotline. For this step, it's critical that the employee information is up to date. The manager on duty needs to be able to access the injured employee's information quickly. If they don't have the employee's ID, birthdate, and other information required by the nurses at urgent care, this could delay treatment. So, having employee information available to the manager on duty so they can call the nurse's hotline and provide them with the information they need is essential for this process to work.

Next, the nurse's hotline generates a reference number and phone number for the employee to call and receive treatment. Also, the nurse's hotline notifies the workers' compensation insurance company. The process of obtaining workers' comp is initiated when the manager on duty calls the nurse's hotline. Through this process, we begin to see how each step in the process is linked to the next and how each step depends on the previous step.

Once the key steps of the process are recorded in the SIPOC, we turn to the inputs, outputs, suppliers, and customers.

Inputs

In this example, the first input identified regarding an incident is some type of injury sustained by an employee. Another example of an input is the information needed for someone to call the nurse's hotline.

Outputs

An output is a result of an action. In this example, one output noted is a notification of the injury to the manager on duty. Another output is a notification from a nurse or HR to the insurance company of a potential workers' compensation claim.

Customers

In the example, the employee, the manager on duty, the nurse's hotline, and the insurance company are all customers. When the incident first occurs, the customers are the manager on duty and the employees because they are the recipients of the inputs or the parties responding to the input. That encapsulates the initial building of the SIPOC. For Step 3, we again look at each of the items or activities on the SIPOC from the perspective of quality, value, and speed.

Step 3. QVS

Process	Quality	Value (Cost)	Speed (Timeliness)
Incident Occurs			Immediately inform manager on duty & perform first aid - As Soon As Possible
Determine if it may be life-threatening or urgent care	If in doubt, dial 911.	Take proper precautions to prioritize safety and health of employee over cost!	If life-threatening, then call 911 immediately. Proceed to call NH once employee is in ambulance
Call Nurses Hotline 888-333-3334 Review annually to confirm no changes	Ensure proper phone number is called by Manager on Duty (MOD)		Immediate - As Soon As Possible
Share reference number & phone number with affected employee	Make sure reference number is repeated & documented	Proper reference number will be required throughout investigation	Immediate - As Soon As Possible

Each step recorded on the SIPOC is automatically carried over to the QVS component by the OPTICS software.

Looking at the first entry in the example once again, which is when the incident occurs, the injured person or whoever witnesses the incident is expected to immediately inform the manager so they can administer first aid. If we consider what is most critical here in terms of QVS, it is speed. What's most critical is that first aid and informing the manager is done immediately. The quality of the action is less important, and although there is a value aspect as far as the value of the employee to the company is concerned, clearly speed is the most vital element here.

The same is true for the next entry or step, which is that the manager on duty must decide if the injury could be life-threatening and an ambulance is needed or if the injury can be treated by urgent care. If the injury is life-threatening, the manager on duty should call 911 immediately.

Now, if the injury can be treated by urgent care, the next step is to call the nurse's hotline. This is a critical step because the injured person needs to be treated by the right urgent care as designated by the hotline. However, now that the injury has not been deemed life-threatening and there is no longer an immediate need for action, value becomes the more critical component for this line item. For example, if the employee goes to another urgent care other than the one designated by the hotline, then the insurance might not cover the treatment, and this could have a significant cost impact on the company.

Later in the process, the company performs a review of the report from the insurance company of the workers' comp claim. For this line item, the quality of the report from the insurance company is the critical factor, not the timing of it. If the report takes an extra two or three days because they are waiting for accurate information from the urgent care clinic, it's not a problem because the quality of the report is what's most important. So, quality is the critical factor for this item, not speed or value.

To recap, the QVS determines where there is a quality element, value element, or speed element associated with the line item on the SIPOC, which helps to prioritize the steps in the process.

Step 4. Accountability Responsibility Matrix (ARM)

Process	Accountable	Responsible	What are they Responsible to do?
Incident Occurs	-MOD -MOD	-All employees -MOD	Employee - Notify Manager on Duty (MOD) MOD - Attend to employee immediately!
Determine if it may be life-threatening or urgent care	-MOD -MOD	-Employees -MOD	Employee - Communicate if possible MOD - Assess / triage with care
Call Nurses Hotline 888-333-3334 Review annually to confirm no changes	-MOD -CEO	-MOD -CEO	MOD - Call Nurses Hotline MOD - Notify CEO of incident
Share reference number & phone number with affected employee	-MOD -MOD	-MOD -MOD	MOD - Share reference number, phone number, and next steps with employee

For the ARM, we look at each line item in the process in terms of who is responsible and who is accountable. When the incident occurs, all employees are responsible for notifying the manager and dialing 911 if necessary. The manager on duty is also responsible for calling 911 if needed.

The difference between accountability and responsibility is that while everyone around is responsible for notifying the manager and dialing 911 if necessary, the manager on duty is accountable for making sure it gets done. The buck stops with the manager, and the manager is the person responsible for making sure the other members of the team do what they are tasked with. For the next item, again, the manager on duty is responsible for determining whether there is a need to call 911 and that the nurse's hotline is called if the injury is to be treated by urgent care.

Going through the line items a little further, the manager on duty is accountable for making sure a call goes to the nurse's hotline if no emergency services are needed. He is also accountable for making sure the nurse's hotline shares the reference number and phone number with the affected employee. The manager on duty might also be responsible and accountable for making sure there is an approved driver to take the employee to urgent care.

The ARM reveals that the CEO is responsible for making sure there is always an approved manager on duty. If there is no manager on duty at the facility, this is a serious gap in the process that urgently needs to be addressed by OPTICS. The way we do that is by creating job breakdowns.

Step 5. Creating the Job Breakdowns

The job breakdowns are detailed work instructions that support the process steps from the SIPOC. Using the line items from the SIPOC, we can create a job breakdown for calling the nurse's hotline. This is a detailed process necessary to make sure the whole workers' comp process functions.

The human resources department is responsible for the inputs for this item, and an employee is assigned the responsibility for making sure the right updated information is given to the manager or the employee. This is essential for the workers' compensation claim process to be initiated. The employee must receive the information they need to visit the urgent care and to claim workman's comp.

The SIPOC looks at the workers' comp claim process from a big-picture perspective initially to determine the overall sequence of events. The job breakdowns are the detailed instructions of what the responsible party needs to do, why, and the things they may need to do it.

Process	Accountable	Responsible	What are they Responsible to do?
Incident Occurs	-MOD -MOD	-All employees -MOD	Employee - Notify Manager on Duty (MOD) MOD - Attend to employee immediately!
Determine if it may be life-threatening or urgent care	-MOD -MOD	-Employees -MOD	Employee - Communicate if possible MOD - Assess / triage with care
Call Nurses Hotline 888-333-3334 Review annually to confirm no changes	-MOD -CEO	-MOD -CEO	MOD - Call Nurses Hotline MOD - Notify CEO of incident
Share reference number & phone number with affected employee	-MOD -MOD	-MOD -MOD	MOD - Share reference number, phone number, and next steps with employee

The job breakdown shows how to call the nurses using a mobile or office phone and why it needs to be done. For example, this job task is important because the employee needs the claim reference number and the urgent care address. Some of these entries may seem obvious, but when staff are in a moment of chaos after an accident, they can rely on the job breakdown to make sure they take the appropriate steps.

The next step in the job breakdown for "Calling the Nurse Hotline" is to ensure the nurse's hotline has the right employee information from the HR employee information database. This is necessary to start the claim process.

The point of the job breakdowns is to document the specific step-by-step process of a task, including the required steps, how they should be done, and why they are important. As we talked about before with the flattening the chicken story, when employees understand why they're supposed to do certain tasks, they're less likely to take shortcuts, more likely to make good suggestions for solid improvements, and more likely to remember critical things. This is especially important when they're in an urgent situation or in the process of doing the task that needs to be performed.

Job Breakdown Name: Call Nurses Hotline

Date created: 2023-10-25

Date approved: 0000-00-00

Author: Maria Liza Palomo

Process owner: Human Resources Manager

Process Description: When an incident occurs, this is the process for calling the nurses hotline to ensure that the employee gets the information that they need in order to visit an urgent care & the workman's comp claim process is started.

1) Call 800-URGENTCARE

- Use mobile phone or available office phone

  Reason for key point: Need to get claim reference number and urgent care address

2) Provide Nurse Hotline with Employee Information

- Get the employee info from the HR employee info database

  Reason for key point: Nurse hotline needs employee info to start the claim process

  Parts/Tools/Link: http://www.employeeinfo.epszone.com

In the preceding screenshot, you will see a link to detailed instructions in the bottom right of the page. The idea is if I am a responder on the nurse's hotline and don't remember the details of what I am supposed to do, I can go to the website and find the job breakdown for the nurse's hotline to find the details of that job task.

If an incident has occurred and an employee must respond to a call to the nurse's hotline, they now have a link to a more detailed job breakdown where they can get the information they need when they need it. It's easy to create more detailed job breakdowns to support the key process steps if necessary.

Ultimately, a link is sent to every employee with a list of their job breakdown showing the tasks they are responsible for, how to carry them out, and why they are critical. The example I have used to explain the first six hours of OPTICS shows quite a straightforward ARM. Following is a more complex one.

Key Process Steps

Incident Occurs

Determine if it may be life threatening or urgent care

Call Nurses Hotline 888-333-3334
Review annually to confirm no changes

Job Breakdown

Call Nurses Hotline   >   Maria Liza Palomo   Active

Add Job Breakdown

No records

Add Job Breakdown

Call Nurses Hotline   >   Maria Liza Palomo   Active

One client has over fifty job breakdowns and all of them are quite detailed. There is a job breakdown for daily productivity reporting, making motor cartridges, and creating a capital purchase order. This company also has a job breakdown for incident reporting.

If an employee clicks on "Secure the Scene for Investigative Reporting," there is more detail about how to do it and why it's important. To conclude, the job breakdowns are basically detailed, step-by-step work instructions and a way to organize and systemize processes.

This is what the first six hours typically look like when I lead an OPTICS session for the first time. My clients have a clear idea of the process(es) examined, what they entail, who is involved, who is accountable, and who is responsible.

More often than not, the first six hours create many "Aha!" moments, where the different parties involved in the process gain clarity and see the gaps that need to be addressed. Also, after the first six hours, clients have a process map that tells them where their gaps are, and they can start to create job breakdowns to bring clarity, simplicity, and alignment.

I understand the whole process so far has been largely a paper and planning exercise; I also realize the challenge is to get your employees to buy into their new job breakdowns and execute the new processes. So, let's talk about that.

For more information on the creation of the OPTICS system, check out the videos and other resource material at www.opticsbook.com.

Step 6. Implementing Changes

The other day I was listening to the radio and a Simon and Garfunkel song came on. It was called "At the Zoo." As I was listening, a line about orangutans not liking changes made me stop in my tracks. The song caught my attention because it encapsulated what I have been trying to say for years about organizational change management.

My first book on change management was called *From Orangutan to Rocket Scientist: How to Lead and Engage Your Team Through an Effective Process.* Why "orangutan?" I'm not using that in a derogatory sense. The orangutan is featured because of something I learned when I visited the Henry Doley Zoo in Omaha, Nebraska, with my twins. They were probably about five years old at the time. I remember we were standing at the orangutan enclosure, and I was reading about Fu Manchu, an orangutan who lived there. This is a real story.

Fu Manchu kept escaping from the cage, and the zookeepers were getting increasingly frustrated.

The head zookeeper thought his team was being careless. He thought perhaps the junior zookeepers were leaving the cages open or unlocked. Then, one day, they saw Fu Manchu at the door, and he was fiddling around with the lock and the handle. All of a sudden, the door popped open. Fu Manchu escaped yet again, followed by all the other orangutans.

They later tranquilized Fu Manchu and found that he had taken a piece of wire from the lighting up above his enclosure, broken it off, and used it to open the lock. Not only that, but he had hidden the wire in his gums, like a retainer, to use later.

When I first started teaching and really engaging in process improvement, I had one PowerPoint slide explaining the three things required for change in an organization: tools, skills, and mindset. Fu Manchu had the tool, the skill, and the mindset to make a change.

My point is that we are all resistant to change, and organizational change is difficult to implement. However, I believe OPTICS provides the tools and the skills for a change in mindset.

There are actionable ways to implement change and address the gaps revealed by OPTICS. Here are five of them:

1. Eliminate unnecessary steps in existing processes and simplify them.
2. Combine or rearrange steps in existing processes.
3. Implement training and mentoring programs for existing employees.
4. Improve onboarding programs and training for new employees.
5. Automate processes using computer systems and artificial intelligence (AI) technology.

One thing to notice is that all the actions an organization takes at this point in the OPTICS system impact people. Ultimately, what improves an organization's performance is having the right people in the right seats, having the right training programs, and making the right process changes that enable people to perform.

OPTICS starts with people and ends with people. It's engaging people, developing them, reorganizing them, and changing your processes so your people perform better.

Workbook: Reader Self-Reflection

After reading through the book, what opportunities have you identified in your business for better-aligned people and processes?

_____

_____

_____

_____

_____

_____

_____

_____

_____

_____

As a next step, check out *opticsbook.com* for more resources to continue your journey.

Key Takeaways

The first six hours of OPTICS deliver the road map for improvements in your processes.

Job breakdowns guide your employees in the new processes and assign accountability.

Training modules, mentorship programs, and onboarding orientation initiatives can ensure employees have the mindset to adopt change.

See the tools you can access now that you've completed OPTICS at learnmore.epsoptics.com.

What's Next for OPTICS?

I hope you have been able to understand more about the OPTICS system and how your organization's performance depends on the alignment of your people and processes, because it doesn't end here.

OPTICS is still evolving. I am currently working on an OPTICS virtual reality (VR) website called P5rocket.com. It's a platform to explore and find new learning VR ideas and options regarding aligning people and processes and improving performance. You can actually launch a rocket in VR and use your phone to look around and explore the space. I plan to add some training modules for visitors to the site.

For organizations with a limited budget, we are creating OPTICS SaaS (software as a service) for self-implementation. Learn more by visiting epsoptics.com to understand the software's capabilities and register to use it. My goal is to make the platform simple and straightforward, so subscribers will not need any assistance or support.

We are also creating an OPTICS community with trained facilitators to assist your organization. The facilitators will walk you through OPTICS and set you up so you can follow the program independently. An implementer can work with you on-site or virtually.

We are also producing training modules and a series of interactive videos for a mobile app so that anybody on your team will be able to learn about OPTICS and how to implement it.

Finally, if you are interested in engaging more with the community or being a guest on the OPTICS in Action! podcast where we spotlight leaders with vision and clarity, please visit podcast.epsoptics.com to learn more!

Learn more at the app.opticssystem.com software platform and mobile app.

Are you ready to launch?
Get Started at www.epsoptics.com

Acknowledgments

I am so thankful for the amazing people I have been introduced to and engaged with in the journey of creating the OPTICS system! I have been hesitant to write the acknowledgments below as so many people have impacted my journey that it will be impossible to name everyone. If you are reading this and your name is not mentioned below, thank you for your support along my journey of learning and growth.

- Thank you to Becky, my wife of over twenty-five years. What an amazing journey we have been on, living and traveling all around the world to experience so many things together, raising our four children, and navigating the opportunities and challenges of life! You have been the encouragement I needed to keep growing in faith, business, and leadership.

- Thank you to our children, Kaitlyn, Kenton, Ethan, and Emma, for joining us on the journey of moves to Kansas, Singapore, Huntley, the Philippines, and New Jersey! We have had amazing and unforgettable experiences together. Jared, we love that you have joined our family and are looking forward to our first grandchild soon!

- Thank you to Jeni Lyon, Ryan Livingston, and the team at Hampton, Lenzini, and Renwick for the opportunity to collaborate over the past few years and learn about the business of surveying, engineering, and environmental services.

- Thank you to Gina Krusinski, Andy Johnson, and the team at Krusinski Construction for engaging EPS over the past few years and trusting me on the journey of creating cross-functional processes to enable your team to have clarity. I learned so much about the world of construction!

- Thank you, Nirel Inman and the team at Chicago Glue and Machine, for being such an important client during COVID and enabling me to learn more about the world of industrial supply chain distribution!

- Thank you to Lindsey and Rafi Bombino for engaging our team at EPS for several years to simplify, document, and execute on processes. Learning about seasonality in the construction services industry has been fun and engaging!

- Thank you to Stan Khanyukov at Real Trucking. Learning about the unique challenges and opportunities in the logistics industry has been most enjoyable.

- Thank you to Eric and Matt Field for collaborating with our team at EPS to solve challenges in manufacturing, tool design and development, and customer service workflows. You have an amazing team and business!

- Thank you to Jake Young for engaging EPS and integrating the OPTICS system to prioritize, document, and lead.

- Thank you, Mark Michelson, for inviting me to emcee the CX Forums where we have collaborated to align people and process for improved client experiences.

- Thank you to Kris Getty for recruiting me for my first job after college. It has been an amazing journey since then with opportunities to live in Singapore and the Philippines and to collaborate with you in various roles over the years.

- Thank you to Mark Whitlock for engaging our team in OPTICS to solve problems in the consumer products distribution business. You have made some amazing introductions and created opportunities for successful outcomes.

- Thank you, Megan Robinson, for being an energetic coach and trainer who asks outstanding leadership questions for self-reflection for myself and our clients.

- Thank you, Tony Ellis, Ryan Falkenstein, Mike Ridgway, Kale Aberegg, and many others at the Aluminum Mill in West Virginia. Early in my consulting journey, I enjoyed learning and growing with your teams, solving problems using 5S. You may notice elements of the Rapid Improvement Event process that engaged your team in eliminating waste, setting expectations for sustainment, and improving safety along the way!

- Thank you, Elaine Kunkle, for providing the opportunity for our family to live and work in the Philippines. Through that experience, I learned leadership, met amazing people, and grew so much.

- Thank you to my parents and in-laws for providing my wife and me with a loving home and a foundation of faith and encouraging me to start my first business.

About the Author

RYAN WEISS is a Christian, husband, father, son, brother, and friend to many. He has over twenty years of success leading teams, programs, and operations to drive business results and profitability. Ryan is an accomplished executive leader with entrepreneurial spirit, backed by proven ability to deliver superior business results across industries, with a strong appreciation for diverse cultures gained through extensive international work experience in more than twenty countries. He has trained thousands of people globally on continuous improvement while keenly observing processes, cultures, and behaviors. This broad experience enabled him to develop a system for accelerated performance that works across all organizations.